Alfred Hitchcock

Filming Our Fears

OXFORD
PORTRAITS

Alfred Hitchcock

Filming Our Fears

Gene Adair

OXFORD
UNIVERSITY PRESS

To my mother and the memory of my father

OXFORD
UNIVERSITY PRESS

Oxford   New York
Auckland Bangkok Buenos Aires Cape Town Chennai Dar es Salaam Delhi
Hong Kong Istanbul Karachi Kolkata Kuala Lumpur Madrid Melbourne Mexico
City Mumbai Nairobi São Paulo Shanghai Singapore Taipei Tokyo Toronto
and an associated company in Berlin

Copyright © 2002 by Gene Adair
Published by Oxford University Press, Inc.
198 Madison Avenue, New York, New York 10016
www.oup.com

Design: Greg Wozney
Layout: Lynn Serra
Picture Research: Lisa Barnett

Library of Congress Cataloging-in-Publication Data
Adair, Gene.
  Alfred Hitchcock : filming our fears / Gene Adair.
     v. cm.
Includes bibliographical references and index.
Contents: 1. The grocer's son from Leytonstone -- 2. A filmmaker's
apprenticeship -- 3. From silents to sound -- 4. Highs and lows -- 5.
England's leading film director -- 6. America calling -- 7. An
Englishman in Hollywood -- 8. The war years and beyond -- 9. Gaining
independence -- 10. A new contract with Paramount -- 11. Three
masterpieces -- 12. A new home at Universal -- 13. Last years and
legacy.
  ISBN 0-19-511967-3 (alk. paper)
  1. Hitchcock, Alfred, 1899- 2. Motion picture producers and
directors--Great Britain--Biography. [1. Hitchcock, Alfred, 1899- 2.
Motion picture producers and directors.] I. Title.
  PN1998.3.H58 A728 2002
  791.43'0233'092--dc21

                                                             2002000695

9 8 7 6 5 4 3 2 1

Printed in the United States of America
on acid-free paper

On the cover: The Master of Suspense composes a shot
Frontispiece: Alfred Hitchcock on the set at Paramount during the 1950s

CONTENTS

Preface:
The Showman and
the Artist

It is a warm evening in the late spring of 1960. Film fans across America flock into theaters and settle into their seats, munching popcorn as they wait for the lights to dim. In each of these movie houses the ritual is the same. The main feature does not begin right away. Instead, an assortment of "trailers"—short promotional films touting the theater's "coming attractions"—fill the screen. These trailers consist mostly of brief snippets from whatever movie is being advertised. The bits of action and dialogue are usually combined with some breathless narration from an unseen announcer, while an array of boldly lettered phrases appear over the images, emphasizing adjectives like "exciting," "romantic," or "spectacular."

On this particular evening, however, one trailer stands out as different from the others. Filmed in black and white, it begins with a wide view of a small, drab motel. A portly man, wearing a dark suit, white shirt and tie, stands in front of the building. Words are superimposed: "The fabulous Mr. Alfred Hitchcock is about to escort you on a tour of the location of his new motion picture, 'PSYCHO.'" But even without this information, the audience would have no trouble recognizing Hitchcock. His round frame, balding head, and distinctive British-accented drawl are instantly familiar from the television mystery series that he hosts every week on the CBS network. Besides, he has long enjoyed a reputation as the movies' "Master of Suspense"— the director of many elegantly crafted thrillers dating back to the 1920s.

As the trailer proceeds, Hitchcock tells the audience that the motel behind him might appear to be harmless but that it "has now become known as the scene of the crime." He pauses for an instant to let that ominous fact sink in. Next, he points out another building, this one an old Victorian house that sits atop a hill behind the motel. It is, he says, "a little more sinister-looking, less innocent than the motel itself," and it was there that "the most dire, horrible events took place."

Psycho *star Anthony Perkins stands beside the sinister-looking house that was one of the film's principal sets. According to Hitchcock, the appearance of the house was true to the film's setting: "The actual locale of the events is in northern California, where that type of house is very common."*

"I think we can go inside," the filmmaker adds, "because the place is up for sale—although I don't know who's going to buy it now."

The tour of the house includes a view of the staircase—the scene of a murder whose ghastly details elicit a mock shudder from Hitchcock—and a visit to the second-floor bedroom where a certain "maniacal woman" lived. "I think some of her clothes are still in the wardrobe," Hitchcock remarks.

Now it is back to the motel and the parlor behind its office—"the favorite spot," we are told, of the woman's son, a young man "you had to feel sorry for."

Hitchcock notes that the son's hobby was taxidermy—"a crow here, an owl there"—and that "an important scene took place in this room." Yet, he hints, something even more important took place in "Cabin Number One." And that, of course, is where he takes the audience for the last stop on his little tour.

Inside the bathroom of the motel cabin, Hitchcock observes, "All tidied up . . . Big difference. You should have seen the blood. The whole place was, well, it's too horrible to describe. Dreadful." Moving toward the shower curtain,

Hitchcock continues: "The murderer, you see, crept in here very silently. . . . The shower was on—there was no sound, and . . . " Hitchcock flings open the curtain. Cut to a close-up of a woman screaming as a violin shrieks on the soundtrack. The title "PSYCHO" flashes on the screen, and the letters split jaggedly apart.

So began the advertising campaign for what would become the most famous thriller in film history. The unusual, six-minute trailer for *Psycho*, playing off Hitchcock's public image as something of a macabre comedian, was hardly the only item in his promotional bag of tricks. To emphasize the story's shocking twists, the director insisted that *Psycho* must be seen "from the beginning"; when the film opened that summer, patrons were refused admission if they showed up at the theater after the feature had started. This policy extended even to critics. Accustomed to viewing movies in special screenings before their release to the general public, newspaper and magazine reviewers were forced to see *Psycho* as part of the regular audience.

Such promotional tactics may have been a bit gimmicky, but they certainly sparked moviegoers' desire to see *Psycho*. And the film itself obviously did not let them down, for it soon became the most commercially successful of all Hitchcock's films. Unfortunately, the teasing showmanship that was used to publicize the picture also reinforced the opinion of many at the time that its maker was only a showman, an entertainer and nothing more. It was widely taken for granted that no serious artist would work in the crime-and-suspense genre. Certainly no artist would even consider making something as horrific as *Psycho* and then go about promoting it in such a frivolous way.

Viewpoints change, however. In the four decades since *Psycho*'s release, countless critics have declared it a key work by a master filmmaker. Its unsettling power and expert technique have inspired hundreds of pages of critical analysis, and it remains among the movies most commonly taught in film courses. Over the years, its combination of violence, sex, and psychological horror, daring for 1960, has inspired dozens of imitations—usually turned out by directors of far less talent, wit, and vision than Alfred Hitchcock.

Before his death in 1980, Hitchcock made a total of 53 feature films. In addition to *Psycho*, his works include such suspense classics as *The 39 Steps*, *The Lady Vanishes*, *Shadow of a Doubt*, *Notorious*, *Rear Window*, *Vertigo*, *North by Northwest*, and *The Birds*. The director often suggested that his talent for stirring audiences' anxieties came from the fact that he himself was full of fears. He claimed to be terrified of getting so much as a traffic ticket, and he maintained an unusually cautious way of living—always following rigid daily routines, always staying in the same hotels and dining in the same restaurants, always claiming that his vision of happiness was a clear, uninterrupted horizon.

Yet despite his devotion to routine and stability, in his work he was ever willing to take on new technical challenges, and his contributions to the ways in which stories are told on film are immeasurable. His ways of composing images, of moving the camera, of placing one shot next to another—all designed to grip his viewers and stir their emotions—were truly masterful.

In his public statements, Hitchcock often lent support to those who saw him only as an entertainer. He frequently said that technique and style were his real interests, that he cared nothing for "content." And yet this claim is contradicted by the films themselves, which show remarkable consistency, over the course of a 50-year career, in their concern with the conflicts between guilt and innocence, trust and suspicion, reality and illusion, order and chaos.

Showman or artist? Alfred Hitchcock was both.

William Hitchcock and his youngest child, Alfred, strike a formal pose outside the family grocery. The future movie director was about seven at the time.

I

THE GROCER'S SON FROM LEYTONSTONE

Alfred Joseph Hitchcock was born on August 13, 1899, in Leytonstone, England, a community on the northeastern edge of London. His father, William Hitchcock, operated a retail and wholesale grocery business specializing in fruits and vegetables. The rooms above the family shop served as living quarters. It was there, at 517 The High Road, that Alfred was born and spent his earliest years under the watchful eye of his mother, Emma.

At the time of Alfred's birth, the family business was thriving, a benefit that came with the area's swelling population. Located about six miles from central London, Leytonstone had once been a sleepy country village well removed from the bustle of the British capital, but that was rapidly changing. Through much of the 19th century, London underwent extraordinary growth. In the 1820s, its population had numbered 1.5 million; by the end of the century, "Greater London"—the core city and surrounding suburbs—contained some 6.5 million inhabitants. Towns like Leytonstone were engulfed by this ever-widening urban sprawl, which some likened to a "cancer" on the face of England. To others, however, London's expansion was part of what made it an endlessly exciting place, a center of culture and activity. Its diverse economy encompassed everything from clothing manufacture to metalworking, from furniture-making to food-processing. And it boasted the world's largest and busiest port. Each day, docks on the River Thames witnessed the heavy traffic of ships bearing goods to and from Britain's far-flung colonies and other distant lands.

It was a great city where many fortunes were made but also one where thousands lived in poverty or just above the poverty line. The Hitchcock family fell between the extremes of wealth and destitution. As small shopkeepers, they were hardly rich but certainly better off than many of their neighbors. London's East End, of which Leytonstone was fast becoming a part, was home to many of the poorer people who had swarmed into the city from other parts of England, from Ireland, and from eastern Europe. Searching for a better life, these people often found subsistence wages and wretched, overcrowded housing.

Escaping that hard lot, William and Emma Hitchcock maintained a well-ordered household in which they tried to shelter their children from the harsher realities of life that lay not far from their own doorstep. They were, by all accounts, decent, reserved, hardworking sorts—a typical lower-middle-class English couple in many ways. In one respect, however, they were unusual. In a predominantly Protestant country, they were staunch Roman Catholics. Attending Mass on Sunday was a regular feature of their family life.

Alfred was the youngest of William and Emma's three children. His two older siblings—William Jr., born in 1890, and Ellen Kathleen (or, as the family called her, "Nellie"), born in 1892—were away at school during much of his growing up. As a result, he never grew close to either of them. Nor did he share the company of children his own age. Pudgy, shy, and unusually quiet, he preferred to amuse himself in solitary games. As he got older, these activities included studying maps, memorizing the schedules of trains and streetcars, and keeping a large wall chart for plotting the positions of British ships around the world.

When Alfred ventured outside the house, it was often to join his father on outings for the family business. Together they would ride a horse-drawn cart through the streets of Leytonstone and the neighboring communities, delivering produce to various customers. At other times, Alfred accompanied William on purchasing trips. "I remember as a child going with him into the countryside, and he would buy a whole field of cabbages," he recalled.

Such excursions were the source of happy memories, but one experience involving his father was not so pleasant. Hitchcock would recount this incident for decades afterward. It happened, he said, when he was about five years old. To punish him for some minor misdeed, his father sent him off to the local police station with a note. Trembling, little Alfred handed the scrap of paper to the officer in charge, who read its instructions, led the boy down a corridor, and locked him in a jail cell for several minutes. "This is what we do to naughty boys!" the policeman warned him sternly.

From that single episode, Hitchcock would claim, arose a lifelong terror of the police. It was a terror that would

At the Leytonstone police station, Hitchcock claimed, he came to know fear first-hand. To punish him for being "naughty," his father had an officer place him in a cell for a few minutes. "It must be said to my credit," Hitchcock once remarked, "that I never wanted to be a policeman."

13

surface time and again in his films, especially those in which the main character is falsely accused of a crime and pursued by the authorities. Whether the incident actually occurred, or whether it was just a colorful fiction that Hitchcock trotted out for interviewers, is impossible to say. Still, the story does suggest that the emotions of fear and anxiety loomed large in his earliest memories.

While strict in their churchgoing and their childrearing methods, the Hitchcocks did enjoy occasional evenings out. Even before he started school, Alfred accompanied his parents to plays and variety shows. These experiences gave him a deep love of the theater and its glamorous world of make-believe, a love that no doubt helped lead him to a career in movies. And, like his professed fear of the police, this affection for playgoing had an obvious influence on the content of his films. Scenes with theatrical settings would be sprinkled throughout his movies, and even more subtly, the influence would affect his characterizations. In many a Hitchcock film, characters engage in role-playing of one sort or another and are often not what they appear to be.

The family moved from Leytonstone to other parts of the East End—to Poplar in 1907 and then to Stepney in 1909—as William Hitchcock expanded his business and opened new shops. To the fruit-and-vegetable stores he already operated, he added a shop selling fresh fish. Thus, when Alfred entered the St. Ignatius College in 1910 (after briefly attending a couple of other Catholic schools), his father's profession was listed as "fishmonger" on the enrollment forms.

St. Ignatius, though called a college, was actually what Americans know as a secondary school. It was located in London's Stamford Hill district and run by Jesuit priests. The Jesuits were noted for their rigorous approach to education, and this included their methods of discipline. Corporal punishment—usually consisting of raps to the knuckles with a hard-rubber cane—was administered regularly. This environment reinforced Alfred's fear of authority. Of the school's punishments, he remembered, "It wasn't done casually, you know. . . . They would tell you to step in and see the father when classes were over. He would then solemnly inscribe your name in the register, together with the indication of the punishment to be inflicted, and you spent the whole day waiting for the sentence to be carried out."

By most accounts, Alfred was only an average, or slightly above-average, student. At age 12, however, after completing his first year at St. Ignatius, he was one of several pupils singled out for special achievement in Latin, English, French, and religious educa-

When Hitchcock was a teenager, going to movies and reading film journals became two of his favorite pastimes.

tion. None of these was his favorite subject, however. That subject, in line with his love of maps and timetables, was geography. But the most valuable lessons he took from the Jesuits had less to do with specific areas of study than with their overall approach to life and learning. "The Jesuits taught me organization, control, and, to some degree, analysis," he said. "Their education is very strict, and orderliness is one of the things that came out of that."

Alfred left St. Ignatius in the summer of 1913. At this point, he recalled, his parents asked him what profession he wanted to pursue. For lack of a better idea, he said that he wished to become an engineer, and soon William and Emma had him taking evening classes in the School of Engineering and Navigation at the University of London. He studied mechanics, electricity, acoustics, and navigation but was not enrolled in any degree program.

The question of a career became more urgent when Alfred's father, who had been in poor health for some time, died in December 1914. Alfred was the only child left at home. His sister had married, and William Jr., who inherited the family business, was on his own as well. To help support himself and his mother, Alfred took a job early in 1915 as a technical clerk at the Henley Telegraph and Cable Company. He had not yet reached his 16th birthday. It is likely that around this time, he and his mother went back to Leytonstone, perhaps to be closer to friends and family.

The Henley firm manufactured electrical cable, and young Hitchcock worked there for about four years. Eventually he became an estimating clerk. This job involved calculating the sizes and voltages of electrical cables needed for particular installations. The work bored him, and he later admitted that he was not especially dedicated to it. He tended to procrastinate when requests for estimates came in. They would pile up on his desk, and then, when he could put them off no longer, he would deal with them in a burst of activity.

Perhaps to distract himself from the tedium of his job, Alfred resumed evening classes at the University of London. But this time, instead of taking courses that might prepare him for a future in engineering, he studied new subjects: economics, political science, and, most significantly, art history and drawing. For apparently the first time, Alfred's artistic impulses began to surface. Soon he was spending many of his spare moments with a pad and pencil, sketching the people and places around him. His art classes and his knack for drawing paid off when he was transferred to Henley's advertising department. Now he had work that he truly enjoyed—preparing layouts and illustrations for advertisements and brochures.

The Henley company also published its own magazine for its employees, and Alfred regularly drew illustrations and caricatures for it. He even tried his hand at writing. For the very first issue of the publication, he penned a little story, less than 350 words long, entitled "Gas." Inspired by the macabre tales of Edgar Allan Poe, one of Alfred's favorite writers, the story describes a woman fleeing in terror through the darkened streets and alleyways of Paris. She is attacked by a mob of vagrants who steal her belongings, tie her up, and throw her into the river so that "the water rats should feast." Then, at the moment of greatest terror, just when she is certain that she is about to drown, the woman wakes up. A dentist tells her, "It's out, Madame. Half a crown, please." The story's title, the reader realizes, refers to the anesthetic the dentist had been using. The woman's adventure has all been a drug-induced hallucination.

He signed the story "Hitch"—a nickname he liked. His parents had called him "Fred," and his classmates at St. Ignatius had labeled him "Cocky." He hated those names, but he was happy to have friends and associates call him "Hitch." They would do so for the rest of his life.

Alfred was little affected by the major event of the era: the First World War (or, as it was known then, the "Great War"). When the conflict erupted in 1914, he was too young for military service, and when he came of age in 1917, he failed the medical examination. Why he failed is unclear, although his weight may have been a factor. He did enlist in the Royal Engineers, but his service mostly consisted of attending evening courses in laying explosive charges. It was training he would never put to use.

At least one episode from the war years left Alfred with a vivid memory. One night, he came home from work in the midst of a German air raid on the city. He arrived at the apartment that he shared with his mother and found the house in chaos. His mother was desperately trying to put her clothes on over her nightgown, all the while uttering prayers. "Outside the window," he remembered, "shrapnel was bursting around a search-lit zeppelin— extraordinary image."

On quieter evenings, he often attended plays just as he had done with his parents several years earlier. But he had also developed an active interest in an entertainment form with a much shorter history: the movies.

This new medium was only a few years older than Alfred was. The first motion picture devices had been developed in the 1880s and 1890s by various technological pioneers such as the American inventor Thomas Alva Edison, his assistant W. K. L. Dickson, and the French brothers Auguste and Louis Lumière. In the early years of the 20th century, movie theaters steadily grew in popularity. Because the tickets were much cheaper than those for live theater, going to motion pictures became a favorite pastime for working-class people around the world. Not surprisingly, the upper classes tended to look down on the movies—an attitude that was especially prevalent in class-conscious England. And certainly, few people at that time thought of calling film an art form.

Still, the movies were like magic to their early audiences. Basil Wright, a documentary filmmaker who was slightly younger than Hitchcock and who also grew up in London, vividly recalled those days in his book *The Long View*: "There survived, by 1915, the melodramas (serial and otherwise), the comedies, the westerns, the travelogues and the super-spectaculars. . . . They were full of dramatic movement. I remember it. A fire brigade! A car chase! A custard pie in full flight! A train smash! . . . They really were convincing, those movies."

Like Wright, Hitchcock was thoroughly captivated by motion pictures—so much so that, in addition to frequenting movie theaters, he became an avid reader of film journals. These were not fan magazines that fed off the glamour of movie stars but, rather, trade publications that detailed the business and technical sides of filmmaking. In 1919, a news item in one of these journals caught his eye: The American company Famous Players–Lasky, the production arm of Paramount Pictures, was opening a branch studio in the Islington district, just north of central London.

Alfred immediately thought about how he might land a job at the new studio. Since this was the era of silent pictures, it occurred to him that with his experience in designing advertisements, he could just as easily be designing title cards. In motion pictures, the term "titles" refers to any written material inserted into a film for explanatory purposes. Nowadays, titles are mainly limited to the opening and closing credits of a movie. During the silent-film years, however, they were used throughout a picture to convey dialogue and to help move the story along: "Came the dawn . . ." and "The next morning . . ." were common examples. In addition to words, these cards usually featured illustrations. In many respects, they were similar to the advertising layouts that Alfred was preparing at Henley's.

The news item about the studio opening also mentioned the plans for its first production: an adaptation of a novel called *The Sorrows of Satan*. Alfred immediately bought a copy of the book, read it, and prepared some sketches—of devils and hellfire—that he thought might be appropriate for the film's titles. He put these drawings into a portfolio of his work and presented them to the head of Famous Players–Lasky's Islington studio. He was told that the company had scrapped plans to film *The Sorrows of Satan* in favor of two other productions: *The Great Day* and *The Call of Youth*. Undeterred, the young Hitchcock returned to his drawing board, produced sketches for the new projects, and was soon back at the studio showing them off.

The Famous Players–Lasky executives were apparently impressed both by Alfred's talent and by his sheer eagerness to break into the movie business. They gave him some part-time work designing titles. He kept his job at Henley's while producing title designs for the studio in his spare time and turning them in every few days.

Near the end of 1920, *The Great Day* and *The Call of Youth* were released, and both proved successful. The studio, pleased with Alfred's work, decided to hire him on a full-time basis. He had just turned 21.

Hitchcock calls for "action" on the set of The Mountain Eagle, *his second film. Among the crew members standing behind him is Alma Reville (right), his assistant director and fiancée.*

2

A FILMMAKER'S APPRENTICESHIP

As Hitchcock discovered, the Famous Players–Lasky studio was a good place to learn the movie business. A keenly observant young man, he quickly familiarized himself with the duties of the key people who worked on each film. The producer typically initiated the project and handled the production's business and financial details. The screenwriter put the story down on paper, shaping the characterizations, the dialogue (such as it was in those days), and the movement of the plot. Once the actual production began, various crew members came into play. One person was in charge of lighting and photography, a position eventually known as cinematographer or director of photography. Then there was the art director, who oversaw the design of the sets and sometimes the costumes. There was the script supervisor (or continuity supervisor), whose job it was to ensure that various details—props, costumes, the positions of actors—matched from one shot to the next. There was the film editor who cut and spliced the assorted pieces of film into a finished product after shooting. And most important of all, there was the director, the individual who oversaw the actors and technicians on the set and whose vision often determined the entire look and "feel" of the film.

Even with such divisions of labor, the studio in Islington proved to be an informal workplace, and as a lower-level employee, Hitchcock found himself doing a bit of everything. At one moment he might be working with the set designers and builders; on another occasion he might be offering his suggestions on a costume design or even rewriting a scene. "Also," he recalled, "I used to be sent out on odd jobs. If they wanted an extra shot of this or that, I'd take out the cameraman and do it."

Many of the studio employees were sent over from Hollywood, apparently because the Famous Players–Lasky executives doubted the abilities of English film technicians. Hitchcock later said that the studio staff was so dominated by Americans, or by people of other nationalities who had worked in America, that he considered himself "American-trained." Among those "training" him was Donald Crisp, a Scottish-born actor and director who had worked in the United States under the great filmmaking pioneer D.W. Griffith. At the Islington studio, Crisp directed several films for which Hitchcock designed the titles.

However, it was another director there, George Fitzmaurice, who probably had a greater influence on Hitchcock's future working methods. Originally a painter, Fitzmaurice made good use of his artist's training when he entered the film business. He became known for preparing and working from "storyboards"—a series of drawings that lay out the action of a movie shot by shot. With such careful preparation, Fitzmaurice knew exactly what he wanted before the actual filming began. Hitchcock's reliance on similar methods of preparation would eventually become legendary.

At this time, Hitchcock would claim, he had no special interest in becoming a director himself. As he told it, his first opportunity to sit in the director's chair came about by accident. During production in 1922 of a film called *Always Tell Your Wife*, the original director, Hugh Croise, left the set over a dispute with Seymour Hicks, the film's producer, writer, and star. Hicks called on Hitchcock to help him complete the picture. Hitchcock's work was so good that, in 1923, he was assigned to direct a comedy short entitled *Number 13*. Unfortunately, preparations for the production had barely begun when the order was given to stop them. As it happened, the Islington studio was in deep financial trouble. *Number 13* was shelved. Not long afterward, Famous Players–Lasky ceased its British operations, although it retained ownership of the equipment and facilities.

The Islington studio did not lie idle, however. Instead of making its own films there, Famous Players–Lasky rented it out to British producers. One young man who took advantage of this arrangement was Michael Balcon. Only three years older than Hitchcock, Balcon had come to London in 1922 from Birmingham, an industrial city about 100 miles northwest of the capital. Balcon and his partner, Victor Saville, produced advertising films for C. M. Woolf, a London-based businessman and financier. The pair now wanted to make feature films for which Woolf would act as distributor.

Michael Balcon, Hitchcock's producer on nine early films, became a giant in the British film industry. Hitchcock once noted that his debt to Balcon was "more than I can say."

During the summer of 1923, Balcon, Saville, and another businessman, John Freedman, rented the Islington studio to produce a film entitled *Woman to Woman*. It told the story of a British officer who has a love affair with a French dancer during World War I and then loses his memory on the battlefield. Complications ensue when, after the war, the dancer shows up with the man's child. To direct the picture, Balcon and his partners hired a former engineer named Graham Cutts, who already had several films to his credit. They made Hitchcock assistant director, but his duties were not limited to that position. Eager for responsibility, Hitchcock offered to write the script and ended up taking on the art director's job as well. His ambition, talent, and versatility impressed his bosses, particularly Balcon.

It was on *Woman to Woman* that Hitchcock first worked closely with his future wife. The producers allowed him to hire other crew members for the project, and to edit the film, he brought in a young woman named Alma Lucy Reville, whom he had met a couple of years earlier. A native of London's West End, Alma had been working in the film business, both as an editor and script supervisor, since she was 16. Although Alma had caught Hitchcock's eye, he had rarely spoken to her before the making of *Woman to Woman*. He later confessed that he had admired her from afar but that he felt uncomfortable about approaching her, at least until he had risen to a position higher than hers. Hitchcock had never really been out with a girl and was, by his own admission, "very shy" around women.

After *Woman to Woman* (which opened to great success late in 1923), Hitchcock and Alma continued to work together on several more features directed by Graham Cutts in 1923 and 1924. Little is known about these films, although their titles—*The White Shadow*, *The Passionate Adventure*, *The Prude's Fall*—would suggest that they were undistinguished melodramas. *The Prude's Fall*, at least, gave the crew a chance to travel in continental Europe. That was where the movie was supposed to have been shot, but Cutts, an irresponsible playboy, dragged everyone from one location to another without obtaining any usable footage. It soon became clear that the project would have to be filmed back in England.

On the return trip Hitchcock asked Alma to marry him. Their ship was tossing in a storm, and Alma had retired to her cabin, overcome with seasickness. Hitchcock, sensing that she might be less inclined to refuse his marriage proposal in this "wretched state," paid her a visit. He made some small talk about the film they had been working on before asking her, in a seemingly off-handed way, the all-important question. "She groaned," Hitchcock said, "nodded her head, and burped. It was one of my greatest scenes—a little weak on dialogue, perhaps, but beautifully staged and not overplayed."

The couple set no immediate wedding date. This was a time when long engagements were common, and Hitchcock probably wanted to rise a bit higher in the film industry before taking on marital responsibilities.

In the meantime, he continued to learn the craft of movie making. His experience during the production of another Cutts film, *The Blackguard*, proved to be especially valuable, even though little of what he learned came from Cutts. *The Blackguard* was a British-German co-production filmed entirely at the Berlin facilities of UFA (Universum Film Aktiengesellschaft). This studio, one of the world's finest and most elaborately equipped, was home to such master directors as Fritz Lang and F. W. Murnau. In fact, while Hitchcock was at UFA, Murnau was busy preparing *The Last Laugh*, which would one day be hailed as a great classic of the silent era. It concerned a proud hotel doorman who is humiliated by his demotion to lavatory attendant. Murnau sought to tell the story entirely in images, without using title cards.

Visiting Murnau's set, Hitchcock was much impressed by the German director's visual virtuosity, which included complex camera movements, dramatic lighting effects, and close attention to background detail. Within the UFA studio confines, Murnau and his set designers created the appearance of a major city. Hitchcock watched as Murnau directed one scene that involved a train's arrival at a station. A full-sized train car stood in the foreground of the shot, with progressively smaller-scale cars arranged behind it. This technique, called "forced perspective," gave the impression of great depth, making the station-house set appear to be much larger than it actually was. Observing the staging of such scenes, Hitchcock absorbed valuable lessons about the creation of movie magic.

He was able to apply what he learned to the making of *The Blackguard*. Although Cutts was supposedly the film's director, Hitchcock often found himself doing much of the work. For one fanciful sequence he had to create a heavenly landscape filled with clouds and hosts of angels. In hiring "extras" (minor performers used in crowd scenes) to play the angels, Hitchcock ingeniously drew on the principle of forced perspective. Very tall persons were chosen for the front rows of angels; people of diminishing height were placed in the rows behind and above them; and, finally, behind the smallest people, costumed dolls were placed. The on-screen illusion was of a huge crowd of angels receding into the horizon.

Hitchcock's obvious talent so impressed Michael Balcon that, in 1925, he was ready to make him a full-fledged director. By this time, Balcon and his partners had purchased the Islington studios and formed their own company, Gainsborough Pictures. However, not everyone there wanted to see Hitchcock succeed. Graham Cutts, for one, had taken a dislike to his younger assistant, probably because he realized that Hitchcock's talent exceeded his own. Also, Balcon's associates were cautious about their money and nervous about promoting so young a man to the all-important job of director. To reduce the risk, Balcon struck a deal with another German company, the Emelka Studios of Munich, to help finance Hitchcock's first picture. The actual shooting would take place in Germany and Italy, far away from those who might thwart Hitchcock's advance up the ranks. Alma was named assistant director for the film, and the two of them left for Germany in early June 1925.

Their assignment was a film called *The Pleasure Garden*. A melodramatic story about the loves and problems of two chorus girls, it starred Virginia Valli, an American actress who was a major star in those days. By hiring a well-known Hollywood player, Balcon hoped to tap successfully into the huge American market. Her stature in the film world intimidated Hitchcock, but he did his best to hide it.

The film required considerable shooting in exterior locations in northern Italy. For Hitchcock, directing these scenes gave him "some of the nastiest shocks in my whole life." The nightmare—or comedy of errors—began in Munich when the leading man left his makeup kit in a taxicab and nearly missed the train to Italy. Then, just as they reached the border crossing, Hitchcock's cameraman advised him against declaring their equipment to customs officials. Unfortunately, this attempt to avoid paying a border tax backfired. Their film stock, 10,000 feet of it, was discovered and confiscated. As a result, they had to pay a stiff fine and purchase new film.

The worst was still to come. The filmmakers had barely arrived at their shooting location when the production's remaining money was stolen from Hitchcock's hotel room. Desperate, Hitchcock borrowed cash from his associates and even wired London for money from his own account. That money evaporated quickly, and Hitchcock's frantic efforts to secure more funds from Munich met with minimal success. The studio would cover only a fraction of their expenses. Hitchcock saw no alternative but to ask Virginia Valli, the pampered American star, for a loan. "But, like a man," he said, "I left Miss Reville to do all the dirty work." Luckily, Alma's mission succeeded: she returned to her future husband with $200 of Virginia Valli's money.

Eventually, the film crew returned to Munich. Here, Hitchcock found himself in more comfortable surround- ings—a studio where he could control conditions. The rest of the filming went smoothly. The experience had one last- ing effect on the director: From then on, he would always prefer the studio to shooting on location.

Before the year was over, Hitchcock would direct anoth- er film in Germany. Entitled *The Mountain Eagle*, it was set in the hills of Kentucky, and centered on an innocent young schoolteacher who tries to escape the unwanted attentions of an evil storekeeper. Hitchcock later remembered it as a terri- ble movie, and he never regretted that all copies of the film disappeared. His next project, however, he would remember in a much different light.

FROM SILENTS
TO SOUND

Back in London when 1926 arrived, Hitchcock had little to do but wait for his next assignment and for the release of the two films he had just completed. Still living with his mother in Leytonstone, he tried to see Alma whenever he could. She was quite busy, however, sometimes working on three or four films at a time in one capacity or another—as editor, writer, or script supervisor. But Hitchcock craved contact with her and so wrote her letters and telephoned her almost daily.

He also found stimulation in meetings of the London Film Society, which a small group of intellectuals had founded the previous year. The Society's members—including such notables as playwright George Bernard Shaw, economist John Maynard Keynes, and author H. G. Wells—saw the cinema as a serious art form, although they generally agreed that British films were sadly inferior to the works of German, Soviet, and American filmmakers. Encouraging greater awareness of "artistic" films was a key goal of the Society, and to do so, it often arranged exhibitions of out-standing foreign pictures. Hitchcock rarely missed such screenings, which became an integral part of his early professional education. While German films taught him much about lighting, composition, and camera movement, those of Soviet and American origin gave him important lessons in the art of editing, of arranging bits of film into meaningful and exciting patterns.

Meanwhile, however, he was growing increasingly anxious about his future as a director. In late March, *The Pleasure Garden* was shown to the press, and despite favorable reviews, C. M. Woolf, Gainsborough's distributor, disliked the film and those "arty" effects Hitchcock had learned from foreign filmmakers. Such touches, in Woolf's opinion, were sure to confuse British audiences. He declined to release either *The Pleasure Garden* or *The Mountain Eagle*. Disheartened, Hitchcock feared that his directing career might be over when it had barely begun.

Hitchcock and Alma Reville visit the English countryside in 1926, the year of their marriage. "She puts up with a lot from me," Hitchcock later said of his wife. "I dare say that any man who names his dog Phillip of Magnesia, as I did, is hard to live with."

Luckily, Balcon soon had a new assignment for him—an adaptation of a Marie Belloc Lowndes novel called *The Lodger*. Hitchcock had seen a play, *Who Is He?*, based on the book and was enthusiastic about making the film. This project would become, in the director's memory, "the first true 'Hitchcock movie.'" The story was inspired by the Jack-the-Ripper murders—the grisly slayings of East End prostitutes that had occurred in 1888 and utterly baffled the police, who never solved the case. Always fascinated by crime, Hitchcock had grown up hearing stories about the notorious serial killer, and his enthusiasm for *The Lodger* was further whetted by his tastes in literature, which included the tales of Poe, the detective stories of G. K. Chesterton, and the spy novels of John Buchan.

In the film scenario, written by Eliot Stannard (who had also scripted Hitchcock's first two films), London is being

29

HITCHCOCK ON THE ENGLISH TASTE FOR CRIME

Interviewed in the early 1970s for a public television series called The Men Who Made the Movies, *Hitchcock offered this explanation for his love of crime stories and criminal intrigue in general, saying in effect, "Blame it on the British!" The Old Bailey, incidentally, is the legendary criminal court building in London, which Hitchcock visited many times.*

One is often asked, "Why do you have a predilection for crime?" and my answer has always been that that is typically an English thing. The English for some reason seem to have more bizarre murders than any other country, and in consequence literature used to treat crime fiction on a very high level—unlike America, where crime literature is second-class literature. If you go back to Conan Doyle, Chesterton—they were all interested in crime as a source of literature. And I think the British more than anyone else are interested in themselves in this, right up to Agatha Christie. I know that one used to read of a famous trial in progress at the Old Bailey and among the spectators was Sir George Somebody, a famous actor or a novelist was there. . . .

There does exist in London today a group called Our Society and they meet every few months above a famous restaurant, in a private room. They have dinner and then go over a previous cause célèbre. And you know who these men are? They are the lawyers in a particular case—both prosecution and defense. Now, they're not satisfied with having practiced the trial in open court and disposed of it, they want to go over it again, they're so interested. Of course, the judge isn't present and it is mainly for the benefit of writers, playwrights and all those sort of people who are their guests for the evening as they rehash the case. They have all the exhibits, photographs and everything. And that strikes me as being, well, so far into the subject that how can you go further except to do a murder yourself?

terrorized by a killer who preys on blonde women and calls himself "the Avenger." One evening, a nameless stranger arrives at the home of a family to rent its spare room. Gradually, the lodger's odd behavior (especially the attention he pays to his landlord's golden-haired daughter) arouses the family members' suspicions. They begin to fear that he might be the Avenger.

As it turns out, the lodger is innocent. He is, in fact, the brother of the killer's first victim, and he has vowed that he will track down his sister's murderer and bring him to justice. Unfortunately, the suspicion that he is the killer leads to his nearly being torn apart by an angry mob. But it all ends happily: The real killer is caught and the lodger wins the hand of the landlord's daughter.

The Lodger was an eerie and atmospheric film—qualities suggested by its subtitle, "A Story of the London Fog." Filled with shadows and stark contrasts of lighting, with inventive camera angles and movements, it displayed techniques that no one had ever seen before in a British picture. For one scene, Hitchcock sought to capture the family's anxiety about their strange guest as he paces restlessly about in his room, one floor above them. The director had the set builders construct a small platform of one-inch-thick plate glass. The camera was placed beneath the structure, shooting upward as Ivor Novello, the actor playing the title role, walked around on the glass. In the film this shot is intercut with shots of the family looking up at the ceiling. The shot depicting the soles of Novello's shoes as he moves back and forth is not, of course, what the family members literally see when they look up; rather, it represents what they imagine as they hear the lodger pacing above them. The shot helps to convey their growing suspicions and awareness of the lodger's strange behavior.

Such creative touches failed to impress C. M. Woolf. In fact, they had the opposite effect when he viewed the film in the late summer of 1926. He called the film "dreadful" and refused to distribute it. To counter Woolf, Balcon sought the help of a gifted young intellectual named Ivor Montagu, who ran a small film company and participated in the London Film Society. Montagu loved *The Lodger*, comparing it favorably to the best of the German and Soviet cinema. He suggested some minor reshooting and reediting to clarify the action, and while Hitchcock balked at first, he soon saw that Montagu's proposals would improve the film. After the changes were made, a press screening was arranged in mid-September. The response was ecstatic. The reviewer for *The Bioscope*, a trade journal, said *The Lodger* was quite possibly "the finest British production ever made." With the film receiving such acclaim, Woolf reluctantly gave in and set a release date for February 1927.

Why did the director, along with so many others, consider *The Lodger* to be the first true Hitchcock picture? The obvious answer is that it was his first film to focus on criminal intrigue and his first to make systematic use of suspense techniques to arouse the audience's emotions. Through most of the film, we in the audience—like the characters in the story—are led to suspect that the lodger is the Avenger, and we fear that the heroine's growing attraction to the mysterious stranger could lead to her death. We only discover the lodger's true identity near the end. At this point, our sympathies shift: Now we fear for the lodger's safety when he is hunted down and almost killed by the mob, which is ignorant of his innocence.

That the lodger is innocent also makes this the first film in which Hitchcock explored the "wrong man" theme. During the movie's planning stage, the director wanted to leave it unclear to the very end whether the lodger is guilty or not. With the casting of Novello in the lead, however, this was out of the question. A well-known "matinee idol" of the period, Novello was simply too popular, the producers believed, for the audience to accept him as a psychopathic murderer. This change in plans, however, opened up the film to other interesting interpretations. While innocent of actual crimes, the lodger apparently harbors guilty desires: he carries a gun he might well use on the Avenger, should the opportunity arise. Although the police find the killer first, we suspect that the lodger intended to take the law into his own hands, acting as self-appointed judge, jury, and executioner. He is thus a "tainted hero"—a figure that would become familiar in Hitchcock's films and perhaps derived from his Catholic background, which insisted on the fallen nature of all human beings. Even good people, in this view, may wish to do bad things.

On a more amusing level, *The Lodger* marked another first. It contained the earliest instance in which Hitchcock makes a brief appearance in his own film. In fact, he shows up in the movie twice—first as a man in a newsroom and then, toward the end of the film, as part of the angry mob. In later films, Hitchcock's cameo appearances became a kind of game he played with the audience: It often seemed as if he were challenging the audience to find him. In *The Lodger*, however, he was simply fulfilling the role of an extra. Such scenes required a number of people to "fill up the frame," and in the low-budget circumstances of early British filmmaking, crew members (even directors) would often step in to help out.

The approaching release of *The Lodger* freed Hitchcock's two earlier films from oblivion. Release dates in 1927 were also set for *The Pleasure Garden* and *The Mountain Eagle*. With this good news, Hitchcock and Alma decided to set the date of their wedding. They were married in a small ceremony on December 2, 1926.

It was a good match. Hitchcock and Alma had similar tastes and backgrounds, although one difference was their religion. Alma was a Protestant, and before marrying Hitchcock, she converted to Catholicism. In their devotion to the movie business, however, they were united from the very start. In fact, if she had not married Hitchcock, Alma might have become a director herself; Balcon, for one, thought she had the talent. Once she did marry "Hitch" (as she always called him), she became his closest professional collaborator for the next two decades, and she remained, for the rest of their life together, the person whose judgment about his pictures Hitchcock trusted most.

The newlyweds chose France and Switzerland for their honeymoon. After a brief sojourn in Paris, they made a scenic train journey to the resort town of St. Moritz in the Swiss Alps, where they stayed at the lavish Palace Hotel. The place enchanted them so much that it became their favorite vacation spot, and for many years they would return there for their wedding anniversary.

Back in England, the couple settled into a comfortable apartment on Cromwell Road in west London. Soon afterward, *The Lodger* met with great success. Hitchcock was hailed as the most promising film director in Great Britain, and suddenly he was quite busy. According to his contract, he owed Balcon and Gainsborough Pictures two more films, which he made in quick succession in 1927. First, there was *Downhill*, based on a play cowritten by his leading actor from *The Lodger*, Ivor Novello, who also starred in the new picture. The story traces the misadventures of a young man who is accused of stealing and whose life goes "downhill" from there. That movie was followed by *Easy Virtue*, an adaptation of a Noël Coward play about a woman whose inability to escape her past wrecks her second marriage. Unfortunately, neither film repeated the commercial success of *The Lodger*.

Rather than renew his contract with Balcon, Hitchcock decided to sign on with another producer, John Maxwell, who headed a company called British International Pictures (BIP). Much larger than Gainsborough, Maxwell's studio could give Hitchcock the luxury of bigger production budgets—and a bigger salary. At BIP, the young director would earn 13,000 pounds a year, or about three times what Balcon had been paying him. Not yet 30 years old, Hitchcock was now the British film industry's highest-paid director.

Hitchcock's first BIP production was called *The Ring*, filmed and released in 1927. It became one of his favorites—

the next true Hitchcock movie, he said, after *The Lodger*. He conceived the story himself and, with help from Alma, wrote the screenplay. It was not a thriller but a boxing story that focused on two fighters in love with one woman. Although the title refers, most obviously, to the boxing arena, Hitchcock loaded the film with images of various other "rings"—most notably a wedding band, representing the love of the boxer whom the heroine chooses to marry, and a bracelet, representing the affections of the other man. In the film's wedding scene, after the groom puts the ring on the bride's finger, the bracelet slips down her wrist to rest next to the ring—a striking visual reminder of the woman's torn emotions and the tensions underlying the story. Using objects in this way—as indicators of the characters' feelings—would become, in future films, one of the defining features of Hitchcock's cinematic style.

Hitchcock continued to polish his craftsmanship in several more silent pictures—*The Farmer's Wife* (1928), *Champagne* (1928), and *The Manxman* (1929)—and although he usually contributed to the stories and screenplays, none of these films were especially personal works. Rather, they were assigned to him by BIP. Hitchcock no doubt chafed at such restraints, for he was beginning to crave greater control over his films. This feeling was evident in a 1927 letter he wrote to the *London Evening News*. "Film directors live with their pictures while they are being made," he noted. "They are their babies, just as much as an author's novel is the offspring of his imagination. And that seems to make it all the more certain that when moving pictures are really artistic they will be created entirely by one man."

The films Hitchcock was making at the time may not have given him the sense of artistic achievement he desired, but events on the home front were more pleasing. While shooting outdoor scenes for *The Farmer's Wife* in the rural areas of Surrey and Devon, the director succumbed to the charms of English country life, and in the spring of 1928, he and Alma bought an eleven-room house in the village of Shamley Green, 30 miles southwest of London. The property included a strip of woodlands and a small cottage near the main house. In the years ahead, on weekends, it would offer the couple welcome relief from the pressures of London.

Meanwhile, in an even more important development, Alma had told her husband that she was pregnant. The baby, a girl they named Patricia Alma, was born on July 7, 1928. In a marriage that would last more than 50 years, she would be the Hitchcocks' only child.

The year 1929 finally brought a directing assignment that Hitchcock welcomed. BIP had purchased the rights to

The breathless wording on this poster advertising Blackmail *("Our mother tongue as it should be—spoken!") makes it clear what a novelty talking pictures were in 1929.*

Charles Bennett's stage hit *Blackmail*, and like *The Lodger*, it was a thriller. The plot involved a London shopgirl who stabs a man to death while fending off his unwanted attentions. Her boyfriend, a Scotland Yard detective, is assigned to the case and finds an incriminating glove at the crime scene. When the detective decides to protect her by covering up the evidence, a man who had seen the girl in the vicinity of the killing tries to squeeze the couple for money. The blackmailer panics at a critical moment, however, and flees the police, eventually falling to his death. He is blamed for the killing, and the girl and the detective must live with their guilty secret.

With a cast led by the Polish-born Anny Ondra, Hitchcock had the film ready for the editing room by April. But just as final preparations were being made, the director received exciting news. The BIP studio had just acquired some audio recording equipment, and John Maxwell felt that *Blackmail* should be reshot with sound.

Sound movies (or "talkies") had first stunned American audiences in the autumn of 1927 with the release of *The Jazz Singer*, starring Al Jolson. Although much of that movie (which followed a young man's rise in show business) was actually shot silent, filmgoers did hear Jolson croon several songs, and to their amazement, the words were synchronized with the movement of his lips on screen. He also spoke a few sentences, including the now-famous lines "Wait a minute, wait a minute—you ain't heard nothin' yet!" The sound of those words brought cheers from audiences.

The early inventors of motion pictures had tried to wed sound to images from the very start, and even silent films were not truly silent, since theaters generally employed musicians—from piano players to full orchestras—to accompany the action on screen. By the mid-1920s, a few experimental shorts were being made with sound, but *The Jazz Singer* was the first feature-length film to use the technology. While some thought sound would be a passing fad, others knew that it would change the movies forever. *The Jazz Singer* did not open in London until nearly a year after its American premiere, but once it did, British producers felt the pressure to make a talkie of their own. The prospect of directing one of his country's earliest sound films stirred Hitchcock's creative juices, and so he returned once more to the *Blackmail* set, equipped this time with microphones and recording equipment.

Right away, he had to overcome a major technical obstacle. Anny Ondra spoke English with a heavy accent, yet she was playing a London shopgirl. Obviously, using her voice was out of the question. The filmmakers could have hired someone else for the role, but that would have been too expensive, requiring them to scrap scenes from the silent version that were otherwise usable. If BIP's sound equipment had been more advanced, the problem might have been solved by "dubbing"—laying in a recording of another actress's voice to replace Ondra's after filming was complete. Yet that, too, was no option, given the primitive state of the technology.

Hitchcock's solution was tricky—risky, even—but in the end, it worked fairly well. He had an English actress, Joan Barry, stand off-camera and speak the character's lines into a microphone. Ondra, meanwhile, performed on-camera, mouthing the words silently and trying to synchronize her lip movements to Barry's line readings. This strategy proved largely successful, and even viewers today are unlikely to notice anything odd about Ondra's dialogue scenes.

Apart from solving that problem, Hitchcock showed great flair and imagination in working with sound for the first time. He demonstrated this most memorably in a scene set on the morning after the homicide. Ondra is having breakfast with her parents while a woman nearby chatters away about the news of the killing. As the guilt-wracked heroine listens, she hears the word "knife" repeated again and again. Finally, all the other words are reduced to a drone, and "knife" is the only word she can distinguish.

Blackmail was also a showcase for Hitchcock's growing visual mastery. Its opening sequence, while having little to do with the main plot, is especially notable for its camerawork. Silent except for music and sound effects, the scene depicts an arrest and interrogation. The very first shot is a close-up of the hub of a spinning wheel, which introduces a speeding police van. Moments later, the police enter a rooming house and sneak up on their suspect, whom they find sprawled on a bed, reading a newspaper. Hitchcock cuts to a shot of the suspect glancing across the room, and the camera follows his gaze to a mirror revealing the detectives. Later, after the man is arrested and interrogated, we see his face dissolve into a giant close-up of his fingerprint.

Thematically, *Blackmail* introduces interesting twists on Hitchcock's concern with guilt and innocence. In *The Lodger*, Hitchcock had given us an "innocent" man with possibly murderous desires. Here, he gives us a woman who in fact kills a man, albeit in self-defense, and who passes on her guilt to her detective boyfriend: Choosing love over duty, he covers up her secret instead of turning her in. Meanwhile, a man who is guilty of blackmail—but innocent of murder—dies because the detective manages to shift suspicion onto him. By the end of the film, the lovers' "triumph" seems hollow indeed. Ondra's character, in particular, is clearly tormented by guilty feelings that will probably haunt her forever.

Released to an enthusiastic response in November 1929, *Blackmail* was Hitchcock's biggest success since *The Lodger*. While he was not yet firmly entrenched in the thriller genre, he obviously had a flair for it.

CHAPTER

HIGHS AND LOWS

The addition of sound to motion pictures left Hitchcock with mixed emotions. He often complained that after sound arrived, too many movies simply became "photographs of people talking"—in other words, filmed theater. While sound offered new creative possibilities of its own, something important was lost, and that, according to Hitchcock, was "the art of reproducing life entirely in pictures."

Too much talk was definitely a problem with his next big assignment from BIP: *Juno and the Paycock* (1930), an adaptation of a drama by the noted Irish playwright Sean O'Casey. Focusing on a family caught in the middle of a political uprising in Ireland, O'Casey's play was heavy on dialogue, with most of its action confined to one room. Consequently, it gave Hitchcock few opportunities, in his words, "of narrating it in cinematic form." When the movie received rave reviews, the director was embarrassed, feeling that he "had stolen something." This experience cemented his conviction that the art of film was more about images than about spoken words.

The visual emphasis that became Hitchcock's hallmark was not something that arose spontaneously on the set during filming. Instead, it was the result of careful planning. Even on his earliest pictures, following the example of George Fitzmaurice, he would sketch out camera angles and outline shot sequences on paper long before the cameras began rolling. Whenever he could, he would also collaborate closely with the writers, developing the screenplay to make sure that it conformed to his wishes. He often said that by the time he got to the set, the truly creative work had already been done, and shooting the film was almost anticlimactic, even boring. On some occasions, especially after he had enjoyed a lunchtime drink or two, he was known to nod off during filming.

After *Juno and the Paycock*, Hitchcock returned to the thriller genre with a film called *Murder!* (1930). Alma wrote the screenplay, adapting it from the novel and play *Enter Sir John* by Clemence Dane and Helen Simpson. The story concerned a famous stage actor, Sir John Menier (Herbert

During his years in the British cinema, Hitchcock often planned his films at his apartment on Cromwell Road in London. Alma, seated here between her husband and a production secretary, was his closest collaborator during this period.

Marshall), who serves on a jury that convicts a young woman of murder. Afterward, driven by lingering feelings that the woman is innocent, Sir John sets out to find the real killer. Much of the ensuing action involves a troupe of actors, which gave Hitchcock, still a passionate playgoer, an appealing background for the story. In an amusing scene early in the film, the police conduct an interrogation backstage while a play is in progress. The officers have to ask their questions as the cast members move on and off the stage, responding to their cues and changing costumes. The theatrical settings allowed Hitchcock to explore a theme he would return to in many later films: the roles people play in life and the ways in which surface appearances can be deceiving.

In one respect, *Murder!* was an unusual type of film for Hitchcock: a "whodunit." In mysteries of this sort, favored by writers like Agatha Christie, the entire plot hinges on identifying the perpetrator of a past crime. For Hitchcock, this kind of structure created more of an intellectual puzzle than an involving tale of suspense, in which a sense of danger is maintained throughout the story. A whodunit might arouse the viewers' interest in seeing the mystery solved and the criminal unmasked, Hitchcock believed, but it would have little effect on their emotions. *Murder!* was thus one of the few whodunits Hitchcock ever made.

Still, while the movie's plot structure might not have pleased the director, making it permitted him to "be cinematic" in ways that his faithful adaptation of *Juno and the Paycock* had not. For example, in an early scene depicting the jury's deliberations, Sir John expresses his doubts about the defendant's guilt, and the other jurors, all of whom are convinced she is guilty, start to confront him with bits of evidence and testimony from the trial. Hitchcock rhythmically cuts between close-ups of Sir John's anxious face and shots of the other jurors. Their repeated question—"Any answer to that, Sir John?"— becomes a chant that effectively punctuates the editing of the sequence. Through Hitchcock's skillful handling of the scene, the viewer can feel the weight of the other jurors' opinions pressing down harder and harder upon Sir John, who finally relents and votes "guilty." The scene ends with a wide shot of the room as the jurors file out with their verdict; Sir John, head lowered, is the last to arise from his chair and leave the room.

Before *Murder!* went into production, the BIP executives had decided that a second version of the picture should be filmed for the German market under the title *Mary*. (Such practices were common in the early days of sound pictures, before dubbing was perfected.) Hitchcock's experiences in Germany several years before had given him a fair command of the language, so it seemed natural to have him direct both versions. This he did, using the same sets but two different groups of actors. To economize, he wanted to keep the scripts of the two versions as close to each other as possible, but he discovered that what worked in the English version fell flat in the German one, particularly the humorous elements. Bits of plot and character that were funny to the British, he said, "were not at all funny to Germans."

Another adaptation of a play—John Galsworthy's *The Skin Game*—was Hitchcock's next project, and it was a talky tale concerning a land dispute between two neighbors. Hitchcock could muster little enthusiasm for it. He completed the production early in 1931 and decided to take his family on a vacation later that same year. Their journey lasted several weeks, taking them on a cruise along the West African coast and then to the Caribbean. Hitchcock returned to London with an idea for a new film; not coincidentally, it was about the misadventures of a naive British couple who take a world cruise. Unfortunately, that film would have to wait while he took on another dreary assignment from BIP.

The studio executives wanted Hitchcock to make a film version of *Number Seventeen*, a successful stage thriller to which they had recently acquired rights. It was just "a cheap melodrama" as far as the director was concerned, a hackneyed story about an undercover detective and a gang of jewel thieves. In preparing the script, Hitchcock and his writers decided to have some fun with this unpromising project by turning it into a spoof. But, as he later admitted, the final product was a confusing fiasco. The only thing he liked about the picture came at the very end: a wild chase sequence that was filmed with miniature models of a bus and train.

While shooting *Number Seventeen* during the day, the director and his wife worked in the evenings on their screenplay about the vacationing couple. The resulting film was called *Rich and Strange*. Although the story was inspired by the Hitchcocks' own recent travels, the journey depicted in the movie proves to be far more disastrous than pleasurable for the couple involved. They find themselves tempted by illicit love affairs, and by the end, they have lost their money, endured a shipwreck, and unknowingly eaten a meal consisting of a slaughtered cat. They return to their dull life in London, sadder and wiser.

The film was a satirical treatment of a theme that would preoccupy Hitchcock in many later films. In thriller after thriller, he would show how chaos intrudes upon the lives of ordinary, middle-class characters. Here he explored the theme in a non-thriller context, and while *Rich and Strange* has since drawn its defenders, it was a critical and commercial flop at the time it was released.

Hitchcock was disheartened by the reception of *Rich and Strange*, a personal project for which he always held a special fondness. Its failure and that of *Number Seventeen* ended his ties to British International Pictures. He acted as producer for a BIP film called *Lord Camber's Ladies* before signing a contract in 1933 with producer Alexander Korda. The year before, the Hungarian-born Korda had formed his own company, London Film Productions, and he would soon become one of the major figures in the British film industry. His planned collaboration with Hitchcock came to nothing, however. When Korda was unable to raise any money for a film, he and Hitchcock agreed to end their contract.

At loose ends, Hitchcock was ready to direct just about anything he was offered. And that offer came from an independent producer named Tom Arnold, who owned the rights to a musical play called *Waltzes from Vienna*, about the famous Strauss family of composer-conductors. This was the most desperate point of his career, and Hitchcock ever after called the film "my lowest ebb." He and the female lead, Jesse Matthews (then a major British singer and star), found that they thoroughly disliked each other. Even worse, the production turned out to be, in Hitchcock's words, "a musical without music." Arnold's low budget kept him from purchasing rights to the songs written for the stage production, and the filmmakers had to get by with the Strauss waltzes, which were free of copyright restrictions and thus could be performed without cost.

Something good came of the experience, however. *Waltzes from Vienna* was shot at the studios of Gaumont-British Pictures, and none other than Michael Balcon was now head of production there. He and Hitchcock quickly renewed their acquaintance. Hitchcock told Balcon about a film story he had worked on at BIP with the writer Charles Bennett, author of the play on which *Blackmail* had been based. This unproduced scenario featured the character of Bulldog Drummond, a crime-solving hero who had first delighted readers in popular novels by "Sapper" (Herman Cyril McNeile). Balcon liked the story, but there was one problem: John Maxwell owned the film rights to the Bulldog Drummond character. At Balcon's urging, Hitchcock bought those rights, which he then resold to Balcon. Shortly afterward, Hitchcock signed a five-picture contract with his old friend.

As Hitchcock and Bennett began reworking their script for Balcon, they dropped the Bulldog Drummond character but kept the basic plot. The story, as it finally emerged with

Peter Lorre (right), as the head of a spy ring, menaces Leslie Banks and Nova Pilbeam (seated, center), in a scene from The Man Who Knew Too Much, *the film that firmly established Hitchcock as the Master of Suspense.*

the help of several other writers, involved a couple who stumble onto an assassination conspiracy during their vacation in St. Moritz. (It was no accident that this setting was the director's own favorite holiday spot.) To keep them quiet, the spies planning the assassination kidnap the couple's daughter. The dramatic climax comes during a concert at London's Royal Albert Hall, where the murder is to take place. At the crucial moment, the mother screams and thereby distracts the assassin, whose bullet only grazes the targeted dignitary. A shoot-out between the spies and police follows, and the parents recover their child. The script, and the film that Hitchcock shot from it during the summer of 1934, came to be called *The Man Who Knew Too Much*.

In casting the movie, Hitchcock chose the Hungarian-born actor Peter Lorre to play the leader of the spies. In 1931, Lorre had stunned international audiences as the monstrous yet pathetic child-murderer in Fritz Lang's classic German film *M*. After making a few more films in Germany, Lorre fled to England in 1933 to escape the oppressive new Nazi regime. Learning of his availability, Hitchcock sought his services at once, for he felt—rightly—that Lorre could convey the perfect combination of charm and menace in the role of head villain. The rest of the cast featured two seasoned stage performers, Leslie Banks and Edna Best, as the beleaguered couple and 14-year-old Nova Pilbeam as their child. Adding to the story's international flavor was French actor Pierre Fresnay as an ill-fated agent who first informs the couple of the assassination plot.

The Man Who Knew Too Much was Hitchcock's 17th feature film as a director and his fifth thriller. But more than any of his previous pictures—more than *The Lodger* or *Blackmail* or *Murder!*—it set the course for his future career. It marked the true beginning of his long reign as the Master of Suspense. The subject matter and tone of the film suited him perfectly. As in *Rich and Strange*, chaos intrudes upon the lives of an ordinary couple, but this time the theme came in a package, both suspenseful and humorous, that audiences would find more compelling.

However, for a few tense days upon completing the picture, Hitchcock found himself wondering—once again—whether audiences would even see his work. As with *The Lodger*, there was an obstacle to the movie's release, and it was the *same* obstacle: C. M. Woolf. Hitchcock's old nemesis was now in charge of distribution for Gaumont-British, and he disliked Hitchcock and his films as much as ever. With Balcon away on business, Woolf took one look at *The Man Who Knew Too Much* and declared it worthless. He was ready to bring in another director to reshoot it. Hitchcock was near despair, and according to one account, he dropped to his knees to beg Woolf to release the film.

Once more, fortunately, an old ally came to Hitchcock's aid. Ivor Montagu, whom Balcon had brought to Gaumont-British as an associate producer, persuaded Woolf to give the film a one-week public screening. Woolf reluctantly agreed, but he put it at the bottom half of a double bill. This attempt to bury the picture failed. Audiences and critics alike loved it, and the film enjoyed a long run. To celebrate, Hitchcock and Bennett both took their families to St. Moritz for the Christmas holiday.

5

ENGLAND'S LEADING
FILM DIRECTOR

Having enjoyed success with a spy melodrama, Hitchcock wanted to make another one right away. In fact, he was already at work on just such a project. For a long time he had been a fan of the novels of John Buchan, a British states-man who wrote espionage thrillers on the side. Hitchcock had first read *The 39 Steps*, one of Buchan's most popular works, around 1920, and for years he had dreamed of film-ing it. Now, during the winter of 1934–35, the time seemed right. He and Charles Bennett fashioned a script together, working on it even during their St. Moritz vacation. The production was ready for the cameras by mid-January.

As much as he admired Buchan's work, Hitchcock felt no special need to adapt it faithfully. After all, it was hardly a literary masterpiece that required reverent treatment, and many of its details, he believed, would not translate well to the screen. Years later, he explained his approach to adapta-tion this way: "What I do is read a story only once, and if I like the basic idea, I just forget all about the book and start to create cinema."

What Hitchcock liked about Buchan's novel was its fast-paced structure and abundance of action. Its hero is a man

Hitchcock's storyboard drawing for an early scene in The 39 Steps *shows how he sometimes used dramatic lighting and deep shadows to heighten a film's mood of danger. He followed this drawing closely in shooting the actual scene.*

named Richard Hannay, who, while visiting London, shelters an adventurer who has uncovered a nefarious conspiracy by foreign agents. When Hannay finds the man murdered in his apartment, he resolves to expose the spies while avoiding their attempts to make him their next victim. Fleeing from London to Scotland, Hannay lands in one tight spot after another. Yet, he always manages to escape, and in the end, he helps to foil the spy ring.

While Hitchcock and Bennett stuck to the rough out-line of the novel, they threw out most of Buchan's plot details and invented a variety of new situations. In their version, for example, Hannay is suspected of the initial murder and actively pursued by the police even as he pursues the spies. This marked a recurrence of the "wrong man" theme that Hitchcock had first explored in *The Lodger*. The film also features a romance that is completely absent from the original novel. In the movie, Hannay falls in with a woman named Pamela who at first resists him, thinking him a murderer, but who ultimately joins forces with him to help thwart the spies. This sort of romantic alliance—in which a man and woman must learn to trust each other before the evil forces can be defeated—would become another familiar motif in Hitchcock's work.

The film is also much funnier than Buchan's novel. Hitchcock believed strongly in mixing humor with suspense, and in *The 39 Steps*, he combined those elements well. Part of the film's humor comes from its witty dialogue. Part of it comes from the parade of delightful British "types" whom Hannay encounters in his adventures—from a boisterous working-class audience at a London music hall to an elderly Scottish lady who runs a country inn, from a pair of underwear salesmen on a train to a milkman who scoffs at Hannay's seemingly wild tales about spies and murder. But most important, the humor comes from the film's headlong pacing and its quick shifts from one situation to another. In one scene, for instance, Hannay escapes from the police by bursting out of a window. A moment later, he blends into a group of Salvation Army marchers. Finally, he ducks into a meeting hall, only to find himself mistaken for the guest speaker. Hitchcock was fond of saying that "movies are life with the dull bits cut out," and there is hardly a dull bit in *The 39 Steps*.

Still, the film would not work so well without the charming performances of its lead actors. As Hannay, Hitchcock cast Robert Donat, an actor he admired for his "natural looks, charm, and personality" as well as for his solid theatrical training. Meanwhile, Madeleine Carroll, an English actress who had lately been working in Hollywood, was lured back to her native country to play Pamela, the woman who becomes entangled in Hannay's dilemma. With her fair hair and sophisticated demeanor, Carroll was one of the earliest examples of "the Hitchcock blonde"—the cool, elegant female character that would become a defining feature of the director's films.

The 39 Steps contained still another feature that Hitchcock's films would make famous: "the MacGuffin." This Scottish-sounding term refers to a story element that is of great concern to the characters but matters little to the audience. Whenever he was asked about the MacGuffin, Hitchcock always told some version of the following tale:

> Two men are on an English train and one says across to the other, "Excuse me, sir, what is that strange-looking package above your head?"
> "Oh, that's a MacGuffin."
> "What's that for?"
> "That's for trapping lions in the Scottish highlands."
> "But there are no lions in the Scottish highlands."
> "Then that's no MacGuffin."

All of this simply meant that the MacGuffin is something unimportant, even absurd. Yet it has to be included in the story because as Hitchcock explained, "the spies must be after *something*." The MacGuffin in *The 39 Steps* consists of government plans for a new fighter airplane. But this secret, while it provides an excuse for the intrigue, could be virtually anything, and it would not make any difference to the audience. The true appeal of *The 39 Steps* comes from Hannay's relationships with the other characters and the amusing and suspenseful situations he encounters as he is chased across the countryside.

"We had a lot of fun making *The 39 Steps*," Hitchcock recalled, but some of that fun came at the actors' expense. Hitchcock was a notorious practical joker, and he could not resist pulling a gag on Donat and Carroll. An important section of the film required the two to be handcuffed together. During the shooting of those scenes, Hitchcock pretended to have lost the key to the handcuffs. Suddenly, Donat and Carroll, who had only just met, found themselves literally

HITCHCOCK ON SUSPENSE

*One of the definitions of suspense is "anxiety arising from an uncertain situation,"
and no one could produce that response in film audiences better than Alfred
Hitchcock. In this excerpt from his appearance in the public television documentary*
The Men Who Made The Movies *(1973), the director talks about the difference between suspense and surprise. The film he refers to in the second paragraph
is* Sabotage *(1936).*

The essential fact is, to get real suspense, you must have information. Now, let's take the old-fashioned bomb [plot]. You and I are
sitting talking, we'll say, about baseball. We're talking for five
minutes. Suddenly a bomb goes off and the audience have a ten-second
terrible shock. Now. Let's take the same situation. Tell the audience at the
beginning that under the table—and show it to them—there's a bomb
and it's going to go off in five minutes. Now we talk baseball. What are
the audience doing? They're saying, "Don't talk about baseball! There's a
bomb under there! Get rid of it!" But they're helpless. They can't jump
out of their seats onto the screen and grab hold of the bomb and throw it
out. But one important factor: if you work the audience up to this
degree, that bomb must never go off and kill anyone. Otherwise, they
will be extremely angry with you.

I made a mistake in an early film by having a long bomb-suspense
thing and I let the bomb go off and kill a little boy. I remember I was at
the press show and a very sophisticated press woman came at me with
raised fists and said, "How dare you do that? I've got a five-year old boy
at home." And she was furious with me. What must happen is that a foot
must touch it and they say, "My God, it's a bomb! Pick it up and throw it
out of the window." The moment it's out of the window, off it goes. But
we inside are safe and sound.

chained together, wondering how they might escape each other. When Hitchcock decided that things had gone far enough, he produced the key. According to one account, the joke went on, rather cruelly, for hours, and by the end of the day the stars were left feeling angry and uncomfortable. However, in Donat's own version of the incident, they were in handcuffs for no more than an hour, and Hitchcock ended the gag when he saw how well the actors were getting along.

Released during the summer of 1935, *The 39 Steps* became Hitchcock's biggest hit to date, not only in England but in the United States as well. He was now, without question, the leading British film director. Enhancing his success was a talent for self-promotion that matched his talent for filmmaking. He continually courted the press by giving interviews to reporters and writing articles for film publications. He craved publicity not so much for its own sake but because he knew it would help him maintain control over his pictures.

By the mid-1930s, Hitchcock felt that he had found his niche as a cinematic storyteller. From this point on, with only a few departures, he would specialize in films of suspense and intrigue. In 1935 and 1936, still working with writer Charles Bennett, he directed two more spy thrillers: *Secret Agent* and *Sabotage*. Both films were darker in tone than either *The Man Who Knew Too Much* or *The 39 Steps*—a possible reflection of the growing unease in Europe that came with the rise of the Nazi regime in Germany.

Secret Agent was based on short stories by W. Somerset Maugham, an English author perhaps best known for his novel *Of Human Bondage*. The stories, which had also inspired a stage play, concerned a British intelligence officer called "Ashenden"—the name is actually part of a false identity his superiors have given him—and drew on Maugham's own experiences in espionage during World War I. In the film, Ashenden (played by the renowned English actor John Gielgud, in one of his earliest screen roles) goes to

Switzerland with orders to track down and kill an enemy spy. Two other agents, played by Madeleine Carroll and Peter Lorre, assist him. The Lorre character, a strange man who calls himself "the General," turns out to be quite unsavory. He is a shameless womanizer who relishes his job as an assassin. Ashenden, however, finds spying to be a nasty business and performs his duties with obvious reluctance.

Filled with comic moments early on, *Secret Agent* takes a disturbing turn in its middle section. Ashenden and the General go after the wrong man. They lure him to a high mountain cliff, and while Ashenden watches from a distance, the General pushes the man over the edge. The real spy, however, turns out to be a handsome, likable American (Robert Young) whom no one had suspected. This use of an attractive villain would become another recurring feature of Hitchcock's films. In *The 39 Steps*, the head spy was a seemingly respectable Englishman called "the Professor," and in future films—*Shadow of a Doubt* and *Strangers on a Train*, for example—the director would also make his villains charismatic charmers. As Hitchcock explained, the villain "has to be charming, attractive. If he weren't, he'd never get near one of his victims." On a deeper level, this manner of characterization is part of a key Hitchcockian theme: the presence of evil in what seems to be the most innocent of circumstances.

Secret Agent presents a grim view of the world. Not only does it feature a villain who puts up an appealing front, thus clouding our sympathies, but it also gives us "heroes" who do evil. They kill an innocent man, albeit by mistake. The film has a happy ending of sorts: Young's character dies in a train wreck, the British military triumphs, and the Gielgud and Carroll characters get married. But it is a happy ending for which a high price has been paid.

An even bleaker perspective reveals itself in Hitchcock's next film, *Sabotage* (based, confusingly enough, on a novel entitled *The Secret Agent* by the British novelist Joseph Conrad). It focuses on a London woman (Sylvia Sidney) who discovers that her husband, a man named Verloc (Oscar Homolka), is a terrorist involved in a conspiracy against the government. After the woman's young brother, Stevie, dies while unknowingly carrying a bomb for Verloc, she kills her husband with a knife, and a friendly detective covers up for her. There is a hint at the end that Mrs. Verloc and the detective might become romantically involved. But again, as in *Secret Agent* and in *Blackmail* several years earlier, the happy ending rings hollow. The acts of destruction that precede it are too devastating.

The film's most disturbing scenes are also its most brilliantly filmed and edited ones. In showing the events leading to Stevie's death, Hitchcock constructed a sequence of nearly unbearable suspense. It begins when Verloc, shadowed by the police and unable to perform the deadly errand himself, gives Stevie a package hiding the bomb and tells him to deliver it to a particular address by 1:30 that afternoon (the bomb is timed to explode at 1:45). Since we know something Stevie does not know, our fears build steadily as the boy encounters a series of delays. After Stevie boards a bus, Hitchcock cuts between shots of the boy playing with another passenger's puppy and shots of various street clocks showing the fateful time approaching. Finally, the moment arrives, and the bus, along with everyone on it, is destroyed amid smoke and flying debris.

Verloc's stabbing is a quieter scene but even more masterfully constructed. Set at the dinner table, it contains almost no dialogue and breaks up the action into a series of carefully chosen shots. Close-ups of Mrs. Verloc's hand on a carving knife alternate with close-ups of her and her husband exchanging glances. The tension builds as Verloc gradually realizes that his wife is thinking about killing him. He moves toward her, only to be impaled on the knife.

Sylvia Sidney, an American actress who was appearing in a British production for the first time, was puzzled by Hitchcock's methods during the dinner-table scene. The

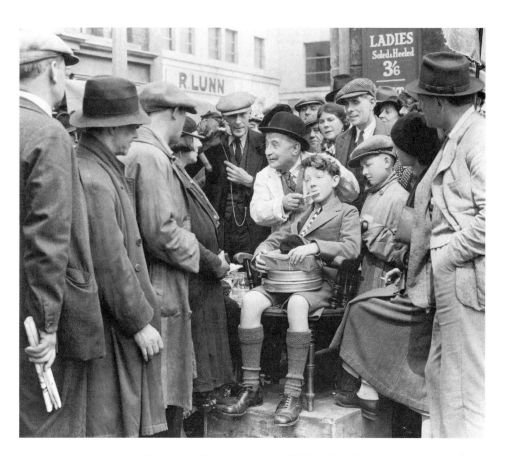

In this scene from Sabotage, Stevie is detained by a salesman who uses the boy to demonstrate his product. The audience knows that the package on Stevie's lap contains a bomb so this otherwise funny moment is filled with tension.

director filmed one small detail of the action and then another, obtaining only the shots he knew he would use. After all, he had already sketched out the sequence on paper. Sidney, however, was accustomed to Hollywood directors who filmed a lot of footage from many angles and left it to the editors to sort out the shots. She could not figure out what Hitchcock was up to, but she was impressed by the final result. "Hollywood must hear of this!" she declared delightedly after viewing the scene.

Not all viewers were delighted with *Sabotage*, however. The bus explosion sequence was too disturbing for many filmgoers, including the critics. C. A. Lejeune, a reviewer for the *London Observer*, felt that Hitchcock had gone too far with the scene and chastised him for it in print. Stung by her criticism, Hitchcock decided that he had indeed miscalculated—even though Stevie's death was crucial to the plot. "The bomb should never have gone off," he said regretfully. "If you build an audience up to that point, the explosion becomes strangely anticlimactic. You work the audience up to such a degree that they need the relief."

A bomb exploded onscreen in *Sabotage*; offscreen, the studio was rocked by a different sort of bombshell. In the summer of 1936, citing financial concerns, the owners of Gaumont-British announced that the company would cease producing films and limit itself to distributing them. Many were fired, and among them was Balcon, who then joined the British branch of the American film company Metro-Goldwyn-Mayer (MGM). Hitchcock, luckily, survived the shakeup with barely a mark. Executives at Gainsborough Pictures, the company Balcon had founded, had ties to Gaumont-British and happily signed the director to a two-picture deal. The films that came of that contract—*Young and Innocent* (1937) and *The Lady Vanishes* (1938)—would be lighter in tone than *Secret Agent* and *Sabotage*, neither of which fared well commercially.

Young and Innocent was a romantic chase thriller in the vein of *The 39 Steps*—but without the spy element. The film concerns a police chief's daughter (Nova Pilbeam, previously seen as the kidnapped child in *The Man Who Knew Too Much*) who aids a young writer (Derrick de Marney) suspected of murder. The pair take a cross-country journey to clear the man's name, falling in love as they search for the real killer and try to elude the police.

This movie would be the last of Hitchcock's British collaborations with Charles Bennett. After working on an early version of the script, Bennett left for Hollywood to write for Universal Pictures. Hitchcock and Bennett would reunite in the United States a few years later, but for the time being the director had lost one of his most valuable colleagues. He brought in several other writers to help him finish the screenplay of *Young and Innocent*.

In the early summer of 1937, before final editing of the movie had begun, Hitchcock took his family, including his mother, on a vacation to Italy. Accompanying the Hitchcocks was a young woman named Joan Harrison. Attractive and well educated, Harrison had been hired as Hitchcock's personal secretary during the production of *The 39 Steps*. Since then, she had begun advising her boss about screenplays and would soon start writing them herself. She would remain one of his closest professional associates for much of his career, as well as a close friend to both him and Alma.

Later that same summer, Harrison joined Hitchcock, Alma, and Patricia on their first visit to the United States. Following closely on the heels of the Italian excursion, this trip took the group to New York City. They saw plays, dined at world-famous restaurants, and made side visits to such places as Washington, D.C. The real purpose of the trip, however, was not sightseeing but business. Hitchcock's British successes—and his flair for publicity—had caught the attention of several Hollywood producers who were interested in his services. They arranged meetings between Hitchcock and their East Coast representatives.

The American producer who showed the most interest was David O. Selznick. A child of the movie business (his father had been a successful independent film distributor), Selznick had held important posts at several major studios—RKO, Paramount, and MGM—before establishing his own independent production company, Selznick International Pictures (SIP), in 1935. A producer known for his close involvement with all the details of filmmaking, he was building a reputation as a creator of big-budget "prestige pictures." He had recently purchased the rights to Margaret Mitchell's best-selling Civil War novel, *Gone with the Wind*, and was planning to turn it into a Technicolor epic. That project, Selznick knew, would consume much of his energy for months, and so for other films he wanted to hire directors who could also act as producers and relieve him of some of the pressure. Hitchcock, who enjoyed a producer's control over his British films (even if others were actually credited in that capacity), seemed like a prime prospect. Accordingly, Kay Brown, who ran Selznick's East Coast office, met with Hitchcock and discussed the possibility of a contract. However, no deal was signed—with Selznick or with anyone else—before Hitchcock left the United States.

When he returned to England in September, Hitchcock put the finishing touches on *Young and Innocent* and considered the possibilities for his next film, the one that would fulfill his Gainsborough contract. He did not find much that excited him until a ready-made project fell into his lap. It was a script by two young writers working for Gainsborough, Frank Launder and Sidney Gilliat. Originally, this comic thriller had been scheduled for filming in 1936 under another director, Roy William Neill. An odd mishap, however, interrupted Neill's production. The assistant director took a crew to Yugoslavia for location shooting and there fractured his ankle. When the police investigating the accident discovered the script, they were not amused with the picture it presented of their country. The Yugoslavian authorities deported the film crew. This incident deflated enthusiasm for the film, which was canceled.

Given a copy of the unproduced screenplay by a Gainsborough executive, Hitchcock found it to his liking and wanted to begin shooting right away. A cast featuring Michael Redgrave (in his first starring role), Margaret Lockwood, and Dame May Whitty was quickly assembled, and filming took place at the old Islington studios where Hitchcock had begun his career. The production was complete by early 1938.

A deft mixture of romance, comedy, and suspense, *The Lady Vanishes* (as the film came to be titled) was a return to the spy genre for Hitchcock—although it had none of the somber tones that marked *Secret Agent* and *Sabotage*. It centers on a young woman (Lockwood) who, while on vacation in the fictitious East European country of "Brandrika," befriends an English governess (Whitty). Later, on a train departing the country, the governess mysteriously disappears, and the heroine can find no one who will admit to having seen her. She has started to doubt her own sanity when a musicologist (Redgrave), traveling on the same train, comes to her aid. Amid the twists and turns that follow, the pair discover that the governess is a British agent trying to smuggle a secret out of the country and that she is being held captive by a band of enemy spies. An exciting shoot-out—reportedly one of Hitchcock's few additions to the script—caps the action of this fast-paced film, and the principal characters all escape to England unscathed.

Hitchcock during the filming of The Lady Vanishes *talks with Margaret Lockwood, the star of the picture. The studio was cramped—only 90 feet long—but Hitchcock made the most of it, and the film was a great success.*

The Lady Vanishes was scheduled for release that autumn, and it would enjoy a huge success. Before that happened, however, the question of whether Hitchcock would work in Hollywood still loomed. Financial instability in the British film industry was making that prospect increasingly attractive to the director. David Selznick remained the Hollywood producer who was most serious about hiring him, and when, early in 1938, a reporter asked Hitchcock about a possible future in America, he replied, "The matter is still in the air. But if I do go to Hollywood, I'd only work for Selznick."

Interestingly enough, Hitchcock already knew Selznick's brother, Myron, who had worked briefly in England years before and who now ran a talent agency in Hollywood. That firm had a London branch, and Hitchcock became one of its clients. He may have believed that his chances of signing a contract with David Selznick might be better if Myron Selznick handled the negotiations.

The deal was finally clinched that summer. The Hitchcocks once more visited the United States, and this time they went all the way to Los Angeles, where the director met David Selznick face-to-face for the first time. Physically, the two men were a study in contrasts. Selznick was a tall, imposing man of boundless energy. Hitchcock, five-foot-eight and weighing almost 300 pounds, was a shy but quietly confident Englishman. Each respected the other's abilities and passion for movies, however, and on July 14 the contract was signed. It guaranteed that Hitchcock would receive $50,000 (a sizable sum in those days) for directing one film, with options to direct four more for even higher fees.

The contract did not specify what the first picture would be, but Hitchcock and Selznick were already considering two possible projects. One was to be a film about the disastrous 1912 voyage of the ocean liner *Titanic*. The other would be an adaptation of *Rebecca*, a forthcoming gothic romance novel by the popular English writer Daphne du Maurier; advance readers predicted that it would become a major bestseller. Hitchcock was lukewarm about the *Titanic* project—although he never said so to Selznick—but *Rebecca* definitely excited him.

Before he could go to America, however, Hitchcock had one more British movie to make. Although he had fulfilled his obligations to Gainsborough, he had agreed to direct a film for an independent producer named Erich Pommer and his partner, the actor Charles Laughton, who also planned to star in the production. Aware of the

The Hitchcocks—Alfred, Alma, and Patricia—aboard the luxury liner Queen Mary *in 1939 on their way to a new life in America. Wherever they went, the family always traveled in style.*

possibility that Hitchcock might film *Rebecca*, Pommer and Laughton snatched up the rights to an earlier du Maurier novel, *Jamaica Inn*.

Set in the early 19th century, the novel concerned a band of thieves who prey on ships off the coast of southwestern England. Two people the director trusted—Sidney Gilliat and Joan Harrison—worked on the script, but the plot was hopeless as far as Hitchcock was concerned. In his view, it was an absurdly structured story in which the identity of the criminal ringleader, Laughton's character, is revealed far too early. "I was truly discouraged," Hitchcock recalled, "but the contract had been signed."

If making the film version of *Jamaica Inn* was a dreary experience, Hitchcock could take heart at two other developments. *The Lady Vanishes* opened in October to rave reviews and tremendous international success. In the United States, the New York Film Critics Circle voted it the best film of the year. Meanwhile, Selznick had purchased the film rights to *Rebecca* and decided that Hitchcock should direct it. At Selznick's instructions, Hitchcock set to work on a "treatment" for the film—a narrative sketch of how the story should unfold on the screen.

The Hitchcocks quickly made plans for their move to the United States. Early in 1939, they sold their Shamley Green country house (while keeping the nearby cottage), gave up the lease on their London apartment, and arranged to ship their belongings to California. On March 1, they boarded the *Queen Mary* for the voyage to New York. Accompanying Hitchcock, Alma, and Patricia were their cook, their maid, and Joan Harrison, by now the director's most valued collaborator apart from Alma. Two pet dogs, a cocker spaniel and a Sealyham terrier, rounded out the party.

6

AN ENGLISHMAN IN HOLLYWOOD

The Hitchcocks and their little entourage reached New York within a few days of leaving England. Since they were not due in Los Angeles for a month, they lingered in Manhattan through most of March, enjoying the plays, sights, and restaurants. Selznick's New York office, meanwhile, made sure that the press paid ample attention to the Hitchcocks' arrival. There was also time for a Florida side trip and a few days of beach and sun—the same sort of climate awaiting them in southern California.

By early April, the Hitchcocks were in Los Angeles, where they moved into a luxurious apartment on Wilshire Boulevard, not far from the Selznick studios. Joan Harrison had a separate apartment in the same building, and her quarters became the base of operations for continuing work on the adaptation of *Rebecca*. Patricia was enrolled in a Catholic day school, and her father regularly drove her to class, as well as to Sunday Mass, in a little English–made car he had purchased. The rest of the Hitchcock party did not adjust so well. "We had indifferent luck with the group," the director remembered. "The maid got homesick and returned to England; the cook left us to become a chiropractor; and it was only through clever ruses that we persuaded the dogs to stay on."

Indeed, Los Angeles and its environs were a far cry from London, and the differences involved more than the perpetual sunshine and streets lined with palm trees. The British film industry to which Hitchcock was accustomed was tiny compared to its American counterpart. Aptly called "dream factories," the biggest Hollywood studios—MGM, Paramount, 20th Century-Fox, Warner Bros., RKO—turned out hundreds of feature films annually. They owned theaters throughout the country and kept "stables" of actors—and directors—under restrictive contracts.

Selznick International Pictures was a different sort of operation. Its facilities, which included 12 sound stages (the huge

At a formal dinner, producer David O. Selznick (left) chats with Hitchcock and Joan Fontaine, the star of Rebecca. When Hitchcock consulted Alma about Fontaine's screen test for Rebecca, she said, "Fontaine is just too coy and simpering to a degree that it is intolerable." Yet Fontaine got the part and eventually an Oscar nomination for her performance.

soundproof rooms where most scenes were shot), were far grander than the British studios with which Hitchcock was familiar but fairly modest by Hollywood standards. Although Selznick had a few stars and creative people, like Hitchcock, under contract, he usually depended on the major companies for "loanouts" from their talent pool. As an independent producer, he generally released his films through a distribution company, United Artists (UA), which made the films available through arrangements with the studio-owned theater chains.

Hitchcock reported to work at SIP on April 10, and shortly afterward, Selznick assigned a new writer, Philip Macdonald, to help put the finishing touches on a treatment for *Rebecca*. Ninety pages of scene-by-scene synopsis—complete with detailed descriptions of shots, angles, and camera movements—hit Selznick's desk on June 3. Hitchcock expected quick approval but got a rude shock instead. On June 13, Selznick responded with a detailed memorandum, totaling nearly 3,000 words, in which he told Hitchcock everything he thought was wrong with the treatment. Years later, the director joked that the memo itself could have been made into a film called "The Longest Story Ever Told." At the time, however, he probably thought it was anything but funny.

Selznick believed that this version of *Rebecca* departed too sharply from the novel, which, as predicted, had become a bestseller. Readers of the book, he argued, would expect to see a faithful adaptation. "We bought *Rebecca* and we intend to make *Rebecca*," he wrote. He complained that Hitchcock and the writers had tampered too much with the main characters by making the hero too forbidding and charmless and the heroine less awkward and timid. He also fumed about Hitchcock's attempts to inject humor into the story. Unwilling to alienate his new employer, Hitchcock dutifully agreed to redo the treatment. The final screenplay was credited to the prize-winning playwright Robert E. Sherwood, best known for such works as *Petrified Forest* and *Abe Lincoln in Illinois*, and Joan Harrison. Although Sherwood got top billing, his contribution mostly involved fixing a sticky problem presented by du Maurier's original plot.

In that plot, an unnamed young woman falls in love with an English aristocrat, Maxim de Winter, thought to be in mourning for his first wife, the beautiful Rebecca. They marry, and Maxim takes his new bride to his family estate of Manderly. Feelings of insecurity soon overwhelm the second Mrs. de Winter, who believes that her husband still loves Rebecca. She is made to feel worse by the diabolical house-keeper, Mrs. Danvers, who was obsessively devoted to Manderly's original mistress. Finally, Maxim surprises his bride by telling her that he actually hated Rebecca—a selfish, promiscuous woman—and that he killed her in a fit of rage and made her death look like an accident. The discovery of Rebecca's body, previously missing, puts Maxim under suspi-cion. Eventually, however, the death is ruled a suicide, and the couple's future is assured. Returning to Manderly after the inquest, Maxim finds the mansion in flames: The fire is the work of Mrs. Danvers, who cannot bear the thought of Maxim and his bride living happily in that house. The house-keeper dies in the blaze.

A plot in which Maxim gets away with murder was something that Hollywood's Production Code—the set of self-imposed rules that governed film content in those days—would simply not permit. Both Hitchcock and Selznick would have preferred to keep this part of the story as it was, but they knew that the industry censors would prevail. Thus, with Sherwood's help, the plot was "fixed": Rebecca's death, in the film version, results from an accident.

Since *Rebecca* was set in England, most of the parts went to British actors. The acclaimed stage performer Judith Anderson played Mrs. Danvers, while George Sanders portrayed Rebecca's roguish cousin; other roles featured various English émigrés to Hollywood, such as Nigel Bruce, C. Aubrey Smith, and Leo G. Carroll. Laurence Olivier, already one of Britain's most distinguished men of the theater and the star of

Hollywood's just-released version of *Wuthering Heights*, was selected to play Maxim. Olivier hoped that his fiancée, Vivien Leigh—who had won the coveted role of Scarlett O'Hara in *Gone with the Wind*—would be cast opposite him. But Selznick, just as he had done with the role of Scarlett, launched a well-publicized "star search" and tested several actresses for the female lead. The 21-year-old Joan Fontaine (whose parents were British although she had been brought up in America) ultimately got the part.

When filming began that autumn, the set was tense for a variety of reasons—not the least of which was the crisis in Europe: Hitler's invasion of Poland on September 1 had led Britain to declare war on Germany. Suddenly, Hitchcock, Alma, and most of the actors were deeply fearful about the fate of their homeland and their relatives. As Olivier put it, "We felt blighted right through." Alma began making plans to bring her mother and sister to America. Hitchcock wanted to do the same with his mother, but she refused to leave England.

As the war preyed on everyone's mind, the filming of *Rebecca* proceeded. Because Selznick was still tinkering with *Gone with the Wind*, he did not supervise Hitchcock as closely as he might have. Several things about the production bothered him, however, and he relayed his concerns to Hitchcock in a deluge of memos. Many of Selznick's complaints were minor, but what truly unnerved him was Hitchcock's seeming ineffi-ciency. Although he tried to avoid a face-to-face confrontation with the director, Selznick told an associate that Hitchcock was "the slowest director we have had." Much of the problem, Selznick admitted, had to do with coaxing a convincing perfor-mance out of an inexperienced female lead. Still, he fretted as the schedule lengthened and the costs mounted. *Rebecca* was originally budgeted at $800,000; before long it was clear that it would cost around $1 million. In 1939 that was a lot of money.

But it was not just the money that irked Selznick—it was Hitchcock's method. The director's careful planning of each angle and camera movement made Selznick fear that he would be unable to dictate the final cut of the film. Despite his stated intention to hire a director who could also act as a producer, Selznick actually hated giving up control.

To reassert his authority over *Rebecca*, Selznick ordered some additional angles, rewrote dialogue, and had Hitchcock reshoot several scenes. For retakes of the final sequence—in which a deranged Mrs. Danvers darts about amid the flames in Rebecca's bedroom—Selznick appeared on the set, and shooting went on well into the early hours of the morning. In the tug-of-war between producer and director over the ending, Selznick did relent on one point: he had wanted the smoke from the burning Manderly to form a giant R in the sky—an idea Hitchcock considered ridiculous. Hitchcock convinced Selznick to settle for a close-up of the fire consuming Rebecca's monogrammed pillowcase.

Originally scheduled for 36 days of filming, *Rebecca* required 63 days to finish. At this point, Selznick took over the picture completely, and to the extent that he could, he shaped the film to his own wishes in the editing room. Not surprisingly, Hitchcock expressed little affection for the film in later years. It was really Selznick's film, he believed, not his.

Despite Hitchcock's feelings, *Rebecca* clearly shows his touch. Using his skillful camera work to lead the viewer's attention to various objects—Rebecca's hairbrush, her address book, her clothing—Hitchcock makes the audience feel the dead woman's presence in a way that a lesser director could not have done. And however much Hitchcock may have grumbled about the movie and Selznick's interference, it did introduce an important new theme to his work—one that he would later explore to great effect in such films as *Vertigo* and *Psycho*. That theme concerns the characters' inability to escape the past and the haunting power that the dead have over the living. Such "psychological ingredients," Hitchcock would admit, began with *Rebecca*.

The film opened in March 1940, just three months after the hugely successful release of *Gone with the Wind*. Widely praised, *Rebecca* became another triumph for Selznick International Pictures. Reviewer Frank Nugent, writing in the *New York Times*, called it "an altogether brilliant film, haunting, suspenseful, handsome and handsomely played." And despite its cost overruns, it ended up showing a profit of $700,000 in its initial release.

Since Selznick had no immediate assignment for Hitchcock after *Rebecca*, he began to loan him out to other Hollywood producers. This arrangement allowed them to purchase Hitchcock's services for a fee that Selznick would split with the director. The first such loanout was to Walter Wanger, another independent producer who released his films through UA. In 1936, Wanger had acquired the rights to *Personal History*, a memoir by journalist Vincent Sheean about his experiences reporting on the darkening events in Europe. Wanger's early attempts to film the material fizzled, but in 1940, spurred by the outbreak of World War II, he decided to try again. Politically liberal and ardently anti-Nazi, Wanger wanted to turn *Personal History* into a timely statement about the European conflict. Hitchcock's British successes with stories of international intrigue made him a natural choice to direct the film. Selznick and Wanger signed the deal for a payment of $5,000 a week (with about half of it going to Hitchcock), and the director began the film after completing his duties on *Rebecca*.

The Wanger project—renamed *Foreign Correspondent*— ultimately had little in common with Sheean's book but a lot in common with movies like *The 39 Steps* and *The Lady Vanishes*. It reunited Hitchcock with screenwriter Charles Bennett, who had come to Hollywood in 1937. Bennett, Hitchcock, and Joan Harrison created a fast-paced story line filled with the kinds of thrills that had marked the director's most popular British work—only now Hitchcock had a budget that allowed him to stage these effects on a grand scale. A fake assassination committed amid a mass of umbrellas on the rain-soaked steps of a government building, a chase culminating inside a windmill, a plane crashing into the ocean—these were but a few of the film's big scenes. The plot that joined these sequences together focused on an American reporter (Joel McCrea) who arrives in Europe in August 1939, just as war is about to erupt. Within hours he uncovers a conspiracy involving a kidnapped diplomat and a secret treaty.

It was an elaborate story, requiring lavish sets to re-create the European locales. To his delight, Hitchcock found that Walter Wanger—in sharp contrast to David Selznick—gave him remarkable freedom in planning and executing the film. He was even allowed control over the final editing. Shot between mid-March and the end of May 1940, *Foreign Correspondent* ended up costing $1.5 million, a half-million dollars more than *Rebecca*.

In late June, Hitchcock briefly returned to England to try to persuade his mother to come to the safety of America. Alma had just brought over her own mother and sister. Nazi bombs were not yet falling on Britain, but that, everyone feared, would come at any time. Mrs. Hitchcock still refused to leave, although her son did convince her to move out of London to the cottage he still owned in Shamley Green.

Back in Hollywood by early July, Hitchcock found that Walter Wanger wanted to incorporate the predicted bombardment of England into *Foreign Correspondent*. A new final scene was hastily written and filmed. In it, the McCrea character delivers an impassioned radio broadcast from a London studio. Outside, bombs are falling. He tells his listeners that "a part of the world is being blown to pieces" and that America "must keep those lights burning." Although the United States was a neutral country at the time, the filmmakers were not

On the set of Foreign Correspondent, *Hitchcock sketches a camera set-up for the film's director of photography, Rudolph Maté. Like Hitchcock and many others in Hollywood, Maté had worked in Europe before coming to America.*

afraid to make their pro-British sympathies obvious. Only a few days after the scene was filmed, the real bombing of Britain began.

In late August, just as *Foreign Correspondent* was about to open, a pronouncement from London stunned Hitchcock. His former colleague, Michael Balcon, singled him out as someone who had "deserted" Britain at a time when "we who are left behind short-handed are trying to harness the films to our great national effort." Understandably angry—and a little defensive—Hitchcock declared that the "British government has only to call on me for my services." Balcon's comments, the director said, could only be the result of personal jealousy. Balcon, he claimed, "apparently hates Hollywood" and resented those British citizens who were working there. The episode caused a rift between Hitchcock and Balcon that took years to close.

Balcon was perhaps unaware that Winston Churchill, the British prime minister, had secretly given his support to his countrymen in Hollywood. Since the war had brought the British motion picture industry to a near standstill, Churchill believed that more good could be done in America, where filmmakers were kept busy. Movies like *Foreign Correspondent*, which supported the British cause, were just the thing Churchill had in mind. And, as the prime minister could only have hoped, American audiences and critics responded well to the film.

Before 1940 was over, Hitchcock had a new directing assignment. That autumn Selznick loaned him out to RKO Pictures for a project that was unlike anything he had done recently. It was a "screwball comedy"—a kind of film that typically focused on a romantic relationship and brimmed with wisecracks and zany situations. The studio already had a finished script—*Mr. & Mrs. Smith* by Norman Krasna—when Hitchcock was hired. He accepted the assignment, a story about a squabbling couple, in part because it allowed him to work with actress Carole Lombard, whom he had met through their mutual agent, Myron Selznick. A delightful performer who lit up such comic classics as *Twentieth Century* (1934) and *Nothing Sacred* (1937), Lombard also made up one-half of Hollywood's most glamorous marriage: she had recently wed Clark Gable, the star of *Gone with the Wind*. Lombard and Gable had become good friends of the Hitchcocks, and for a year, the actress had been renting her house to the director and his family while she and Gable lived on a ranch outside Los Angeles.

Although he enjoyed directing Lombard, Hitchcock later dismissed *Mr. & Mrs. Smith* as merely a favor to the actress. He did not really understand the characters, he said, so he shot Krasna's screenplay as it was written. But the project also gave him the chance to prove that he could work quickly. His first two American features, *Rebecca* and *Foreign Correspondent,* had exceeded their production schedules as well as their budgets, and Hitchcock was probably anxious to allay any suspicion among producers who might hire him that he was more trouble than he was worth.

Whatever the director's anxieties, his American career was off to a rousing start. Early in 1941, the Academy of Motion Picture Arts and Sciences announced the nominations for its annual awards, nicknamed the Oscars. *Rebecca* received nominations in 11 categories, while *Foreign Correspondent* earned 6 nominations. These were accomplishments of which any filmmaker could be proud.

Unfortunately, when the awards were handed out, Hitchcock was passed over. Although *Rebecca* won the Best Picture award, the honor went to Selznick as it had the previous year when *Gone with the Wind* won Best Picture. The directing Oscar went to John Ford for *The Grapes of Wrath*. Being slighted by the Academy would become an all-too-familiar occurrence in Hitchcock's career. Although he would be nominated for several more Oscars in the years to come, the actual award—and the recognition from his peers that it implied—would always elude him.

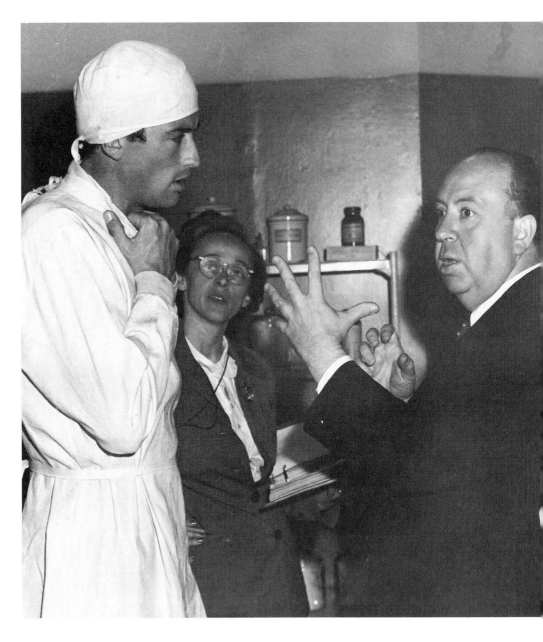

Hitchcock directs Gregory Peck, clad in surgical garb for his role in Spellbound. *In the movie's twist-filled plot, Peck is an amnesia victim who assumes the identity of a murdered man.*

CHAPTER

7

THE WAR YEARS AND BEYOND

For David O. Selznick, the twin triumphs of *Gone with the Wind* and *Rebecca* came with a high price tag. The strain of producing those films had thoroughly exhausted him, and their profits had created a staggering tax burden for both him and his company. In August 1940, to help ease that burden, Selznick International Pictures was dissolved. The producer promptly formed a new company, David O. Selznick Productions, but he decided for the time being to concentrate on loaning out his employees instead of initiating new blockbusters.

For Alfred Hitchcock, the loanouts meant a steady stream of work. After completing *Mr. & Mrs. Smith*, he directed a second RKO picture, *Suspicion*, filmed early in 1941 and released late that year. A romantic thriller reminiscent of *Rebecca*, the movie reunited him with Joan Fontaine and introduced him to Cary Grant, who would become one of his favorite leading men. Set in England, it centered on a young woman (Fontaine) who suspects that her charming rogue of a husband (Grant) is plotting to kill her for insurance money.

Even as *Suspicion* was being filmed, Hitchcock began developing his next project. Called *Saboteur* (a title that often gets it confused with 1935's *Sabotage*), it was eventually sold to an independent producer named Lloyd Thompson, who put it into production at Universal Pictures late in 1941. While the story was yet another reworking of *The 39 Steps*, it was at least timely. The Japanese bombing of Pearl Harbor on December 7 had brought the United States into World War II, and *Saboteur*, accordingly, was set against the backdrop of an America in crisis. It concerned a defense-industry worker who flees the authorities after being falsely accused of setting fire to the plant where he works. Maintaining a patriotic tone throughout, the movie ends atop the Statue of Liberty with a struggle between the hero (Robert Cummings) and the real arsonist (Norman Lloyd).

During that winter of 1941–42, the Hitchcocks saw a flurry of changes in their personal lives. Joan Harrison decided to leave Hitchcock's employ for a career as an independent producer. Although they would get back together years later, at the time of her departure Hitchcock was distraught. Meanwhile, the theatrical bug had bitten 13-year-old Patricia, and through her father's connections, she won a role in a Broadway play called *Solitaire*. Although the production closed after only three weeks, it convinced Patricia to become an actress. Another event, one that deeply saddened the family, was the death of Carole Lombard. While on a tour in support of the war effort, the actress was killed in a plane crash.

After Lombard died, the Hitchcocks could no longer rent her house so they began searching for one of their own. In the spring of 1942, for $40,000, they bought a place in the same fashionable neighborhood of Bel-Air. Located at 10957 Bellagio Road, it was a cozy little house of white-painted brick, surrounded by trees. It had no swimming pool—a feature usually required by Hollywood types—but Hitchcock cared nothing about that. For the food-loving filmmaker, a good kitchen was the important thing. The only disturbances to the home's quiet seclusion came from a nearby golf course:

small white balls regularly
pelted the Hitchcocks' yard.

As the Hitchcocks were
settling into their new home,
the director's next film was
in development. It would
be his most "American"
to date. Writer Gordon
McDonell, the husband of
one of Selznick's employees,
came up with the idea—one
that would dramatize the
intrusion of evil into a small-
town family. In the story that
resulted, the evil arrives in the
form of a visiting uncle on
the run from the police.

*Alma Hitchcock and
Joan Harrison, the
trusted assistant who
accompanied the director
and his family to
America, pore over the
script for* Suspicion.
*Soon after, Harrison left
Hitchcock's employ to
become a screenwriter and
independent producer.*

Unbeknownst to the family, the uncle is a serial killer who
preys on wealthy widows. His oldest niece—who shares his
name, Charlie—thinks he is "the most wonderful person in
the world." Gradually she learns his terrible secret but cannot
tell anyone because the truth would devastate her mother. The
uncle tries several times to kill his niece and, in his last attempt,
falls to his death in front of a train.

Originally called "Uncle Charlie," the film would be
released as *Shadow of a Doubt.* Jack Skirball, an associate producer on *Saboteur,* served as producer for this project, and like
Saboteur, the film was made for Universal Pictures. *Shadow of
a Doubt* became a personal favorite of the director's, and it
certainly ranks among his richest works of the 1940s. Part of
its richness lies in its realistic depiction of American life,
especially the look and feel of a small town and the ways in
which family members behave with each other. To get the
authenticity he wanted, Hitchcock hired playwright
Thornton Wilder, the Pulitzer Prize–winning author of *Our
Town,* to help write the screenplay. He then shot much of the

film on location in the northern California town of Santa Rosa. For once, the studio would not suffice.

Beyond its realism, *Shadow of a Doubt* is a well-structured film about the duality of human nature. The two Charlies, niece and uncle, are said to be "like twins" and they have an almost psychic connection with each other. Young Charlie is attracted to the life of adventure she thinks her uncle has led; he longs for the simplicity of her small-town ways. They are "doubles," mirror images of each other—one naive and innocent, the other worldly and corrupt.

In the roles of niece and uncle, Hitchcock was well served by Teresa Wright and Joseph Cotten. Twenty-four years old (but looking younger), Wright was the perfect "girl next door." In the film, she projects a fresh vitality that makes her disillusionment with her uncle truly heartbreaking. Cotten, meanwhile, is all smoothness and charm until, at odd moments, his true nature erupts. In a dinner-table scene, he speaks with chilling intensity of how much he hates rich widows: "You see these women everywhere—useless women, eating the money, drinking the money, smelling of money!"

The director got along well with his cast, and he was so entranced by northern California that he bought a Spanish-style country home near Santa Cruz, just south of San Francisco. Like his Shamley Green estate in England, this second home became a favorite weekend retreat. The filming of *Shadow of a Doubt* might well have been one of the happier times in his life—but for one thing. Back in England, his mother was seriously ill, suffering from kidney and intestinal problems. Hitchcock regularly received troubling reports about her health from his brother, William. Interestingly, the director's concern over his mother found its way into the movie he was making: the mother in *Shadow of a Doubt* was, like Mrs. Hitchcock, named Emma. In late September, while interior scenes were being shot at Universal, Hitchcock learned that his mother had died. The war and his schedule prevented him from attending the funeral. The following January, shortly before *Shadow of a Doubt* opened, he received word that William was also dead, an apparent suicide.

Hitchcock was an intensely private man, a "loner" by his own admission. He rarely discussed his family in public, and after the deaths of his mother and brother, probably no one but Alma knew what he was feeling. To the world outside, he maintained his professional cool and went on working.

By early 1943, Selznick had loaned him out to 20th Century-Fox, and for this picture, Hitchcock wanted to take on a special technical challenge—shooting a movie within the tight confines of a single set. The story, he decided, should take place on a lifeboat and deal with the survivors of a torpedoed merchant vessel and the conflicts that arise when they are joined by a German submarine captain.

Hitchcock had enjoyed working with Thornton Wilder on *Shadow of a Doubt*, and he hoped to involve another big-name writer in this wartime drama. When his first choice, the acclaimed novelist Ernest Hemingway, declined, Hitchcock enlisted the services of John Steinbeck, author of *The Grapes of Wrath*. Their personalities clashed, however: Steinbeck considered Hitchcock an "English middle-class snob" and left the project after producing a sketchy plot treatment. Another novelist, MacKinlay Kantor, then wrote a script that Hitchcock thoroughly disliked. Finally, a veteran Hollywood writer named Jo Swerling produced a usable screenplay.

If Hitchcock wanted a technical challenge, he got it with *Lifeboat* (as the film was called). Shooting took place in a studio tank with projected backdrops of the horizon. Even in these controlled conditions, however, filming on water was difficult, and the cast members, led by the flamboyant actress Tallulah Bankhead, were often drenched. Hitchcock had an especially hard time coming up with a way to make his traditional cameo appearance. He typically showed up briefly in his films as a passerby in a street scene, but how could he do that in this oceanic setting? Luckily, he found a clever solution: his image appears in a newspaper read by one of the characters—as "before-and-after" pictures advertising a fictional weight-loss product called "Reduco." This unusual cameo immortalized the director's recent diet, which had allowed him to shed 100 pounds. "The role was a great hit," Hitchcock remembered. "I was literally submerged by letters from fat people who wanted to know where and how they could get Reduco."

After the filming of *Lifeboat* was completed in December, Hitchcock returned to England for several months. His trip came mainly at the urging of Sidney Bernstein, an old acquaintance who now headed the film section of the British Ministry of Information. Bernstein had been corresponding with Hitchcock for some time about the director's coming to England to make short propaganda films on behalf of the war effort. He eventually did direct two such films. Bernstein also wanted to discuss the possibility, once the war was over, of their forming a production company together—one that would make films in both London and Hollywood.

During his visit to London, the director was shocked to see the bomb damage to his native city and how the war had all but shut down the British film industry. His spirits brightened only when he and Bernstein talked about making films together. Hitchcock had a grudging respect for David Selznick, but he longed to be his own producer. Bernstein's proposals promised that kind of creative freedom.

In the meantime, however, there was a new Selznick project in the works. After four years and six loanouts to other producers, this would be their first collaboration since *Rebecca*. Selznick was interested in psychiatry and psycho-analysis (a form of therapy founded by Sigmund Freud) and thought they would make good material for a Hitchcock film. While in London, Hitchcock purchased the rights to a 1927 novel, *The House of Doctor Edwardes* by Francis Beeding. He worked with Angus MacPhail, a British writer and his old friend, on a treatment incorporating the psychiatric details Selznick wanted. Back in the United States, he resold the rights to Selznick, who in turn hired veteran writer Ben Hecht to work with Hitchcock on the screenplay.

Hecht and Hitchcock got along well, and during the spring of 1944 they refashioned Beeding's novel into a romantic vehicle for two of Selznick's rising stars: Swedish-born Ingrid Bergman and all-American Gregory Peck. The picture, which was shot during the autumn of 1944 and eventually renamed *Spellbound*, centered on an amnesia victim (Peck) who assumes the identity of a mental hospital director. In a twist-filled story involving murder and false accusations, the hero is finally cured of his mental disturbances by a beautiful psychiatrist (Bergman).

Although *Spellbound* was complete by the end of February 1945, it would not be released until that autumn. Meanwhile, in early May, the war in Europe ended with the defeat of Germany. Hitchcock returned to London that summer to renew his talks with Sidney Bernstein about their planned production company. Also, at Bernstein's request, the director offered advice on the editing of documentary footage shot in the German concentration camps following their liberation by the Allied forces. This filmed chronicle of the Holocaust was so horrific that it remained in archives, unseen, until 1985, when it was shown on British television. Hitchcock, for his part, never talked about it, apparently because the images had so disturbed him.

On October 31, *Spellbound* finally opened in a New York premiere that promoted the sale of Victory Bonds—savings certificates issued by the government to help pay for the costs of the war. After that opening, *Spellbound* went on to strike gold at the box office and garner good reviews, not to mention six Oscar nominations. It became Hitchcock's biggest hit to date and one of Hollywood's top moneymakers of the 1940s. Despite its initial success, however, the film has not aged well. Its psychiatric details, innovative at the time, now seem corny and naive. Hitchcock never counted it among his favorite works. Years after its release, he dismissed the picture as nothing but a manhunt story cloaked in "pseudo-psychoanalysis."

If *Spellbound* would date badly, the project that followed it would become one of his most enduring classics. The germ of the plot was found in a *Saturday Evening Post* short story about a woman who fears that her marriage plans will be ruined if her fiancé discovers a secret from her past: years before, while working for the government, she had become the lover of an enemy agent in order to steal secrets from him. Although the story itself appealed little to Hitchcock, its premise—sleeping with the enemy—intrigued him.

It intrigued Selznick as well. He again hired Ben Hecht to help shape Hitchcock's ideas into a dramatic script. The director and writer worked on the story, which they soon named *Notorious*, throughout the first half of 1945, submitting their drafts to Selznick and then rewriting them after the producer had his say. But even though Selznick was deeply involved in the scripting, he was not sure he wanted to produce the picture. He had another big film in progress, an epic western called *Duel in the Sun*, which was putting his company into deep financial trouble. Maybe, Selznick thought, he should sell *Notorious* to another studio and thus ease the mounting debts.

Ease them he did. That summer, for $800,000 and a 50 percent share of the profits, Selznick sold *Notorious* to RKO. The package included the screenplay, Hitchcock's services, and the two big stars—Bergman and Cary Grant—who would play the leads. Hitchcock got little money from the deal, but it allowed him to act as producer. It was one more step toward the independence he craved. To please Hitchcock, RKO put a clause in the sale agreement explicitly barring Selznick from having any further say in the production. Of course, Selznick, being Selznick, had trouble staying quiet, especially since he owned half of the potential profits. Having a vested interest in the film's success, he continued to offer advice on the script and casting until filming finally began in October.

The film that emerged from this collaboration was an all-round triumph. The reviews were good; the responses of audiences even better. And in the years since its opening in August 1946, most of Hitchcock's admirers see *Notorious* as one of his very best films. Tightly constructed and expertly directed, it is a compelling tale about love, duty, trust, and betrayal.

The film's "notorious" figure is Alicia Huberman (Bergman), the daughter of a convicted Nazi spy. Because of her father's associations and her own reputation as a "loose woman," she is recruited by an American agent named Devlin (Grant) to infiltrate a group of Nazis who have fled to Brazil after Germany's defeat and are now planning a postwar comeback. Alicia agrees to the assignment and soon falls in love with Devlin, who remains coolly non-committal. In Rio de Janeiro, under Devlin's watchful eye, Alicia renews her acquaintance with Alex Sebastien (Claude Rains), an old friend of her father's who is now harboring the Nazis. Sebastien falls hard for her and proposes marriage. Her American superiors see this as a perfect way to find out what the Nazis are plotting. While keeping his feelings from Alicia, Devlin expresses disgust at the scheme but agrees to let it go forward anyway.

After Alicia marries Sebastien, she helps Devlin sneak into her husband's wine cellar, where they discover uranium particles hidden in a wine bottle: the Nazis, it seems, are working on an atom bomb. But Sebastien soon discovers his wife's duplicity. At the urging of his domineering mother, he starts to poison her, knowing that if his Nazi pals discover Alicia's true identity, they will kill him. Devlin finally rescues Alicia, horribly sick from the poisoning, and leaves Sebastien in the hands of the Nazis, who have begun to suspect his secret just as the hero and heroine speed away.

Why does *Notorious* work so well? The combined star power of Ingrid Bergman and Cary Grant and the relationship they portray account for much of its appeal. The chemistry between the two is obvious from the start, but then, for much of the film, their characters struggle with misunderstandings and lack of trust. Devlin wants Alicia to refuse her assignment of seducing Sebastien; she, on the other hand, wants Devlin to intervene on her behalf and tell their superiors that she is the wrong girl for the job. Once a playgirl with a drinking problem, Alicia has been redeemed by her love for Devlin. But he cannot quite believe she has changed until the very end, when he puts his own life at risk to save hers.

Another remarkable feature of the film is its handling of Sebastien. He is not merely a charming villain but a sympathetic one. It was Selznick, in an inspired piece of advice, who suggested Claude Rains for the part. Rains brought a genuine humanity to the role, deepening and complicating the film's emotional impact. Rains's Sebastien clearly loves Alicia—perhaps more than Devlin does—which gives her betrayal of him a tragic dimension. And at the conclusion, Hitchcock's camera does not follow Devlin and Alicia to their happy ending; it stays with Sebastien as he walks to his doom.

Finally, *Notorious* reveals Hitchcock in top form as a visual artist. As his own producer, he was able to film and edit the movie exactly as he wanted. One of its virtuoso moments occurs at a party where Alicia slips Devlin the key to the wine cellar. As the party scene begins, Hitchcock's camera looks down from a high angle, panning across the vastness of Sebastien's mansion while the guests mill about. Slowly the camera descends toward Alicia. Closer and closer it comes until her hand fills the screen. There we see the key gripped between her fingers. His aim here, Hitchcock explained, was to make a single, forceful, visual statement: "In this crowded atmosphere there is a very vital item, the crux of everything."

After the happy experience of *Notorious* came a cinematic catastrophe, the result of Selznick's decision to revive one his old projects. More than a decade earlier, the producer had tried unsuccessfully to make an adaptation of a 1933 English novel called *The Paradine Case*. It was a courtroom drama about a London defense attorney who falls in love with his beautiful, guilty client. Selznick offered it to Hitchcock in 1946. Although he itched to start a partnership with Bernstein, Hitchcock owed Selznick one last picture. The British setting and mysterious woman at the heart of the story exerted some appeal, and he agreed to direct it. He regretted it ever afterward.

When early attempts to shape the script faltered, Selznick took over the writing himself. He continued working on the screenplay after production began in December. As Hitchcock recalled, Selznick sent new pages of the script to the set every couple of days—a method of work that was naturally exasperating to someone with Hitchcock's sense of order and love for advance planning.

Compounding the script problems was unfortunate casting. In the role of the obsessed lawyer, Gregory Peck tried valiantly, and with no success, to imitate a British accent. As the defendant, the Italian actress Alida Valli was exotic-looking, yet cold and distant. Most disastrous, Hitchcock believed, was the young French actor Louis Jourdan as a stable hand whom Peck tries to implicate in the murder with which his client has been charged. This part, Hitchcock believed, needed someone who looked as if he smelled of horse manure; Jourdan was far too suave and good-looking.

The supporting actors—Charles Laughton, Ann Todd, Ethel Barrymore—fared a bit better. In particular, Laughton's performance as a lecherous judge is fun to watch. Yet even he could barely enliven what was basically a talky, static picture with miscast leads. Despite a big marketing push from Selznick, the film flopped when it was released in December 1947. It took $4 million to make—the highest cost yet for a Hitchcock film—and it made only $2.2 million in return.

It did, however, relieve Hitchcock of his obligations to Selznick. A freer future now awaited him as he joined forces with Sidney Bernstein.

In 1948, Ingrid Bergman and Hitchcock enjoy sightseeing in London during a break in the filming of Under Capricorn. *This spot on the edge of the River Thames, with the Houses of Parliament in the background, became the location, 23 years later, for the opening scene of the director's 52nd film,* Frenzy.

GAINING INDEPENDENCE

Hitchcock and Bernstein called their new production company Transatlantic Pictures—an appropriate name since they planned to make movies in both England and the United States. After approaching several studios, they reached an agreement with Warner Bros. for distribution. Unfortunately, despite the hopes of Transatlantic's founders, only two films would come of the partnership: *Rope* (1948) and *Under Capricorn* (1949).

Under Capricorn was conceived as a vehicle for Ingrid Bergman and was supposed to have been filmed first. The actress had other commitments, however, so Hitchcock and Bernstein decided to do something that could be shot quickly. They settled on adapting a play, Patrick Hamilton's *Rope*, which they had both seen during its London run in 1929.

The story was loosely derived from an actual case involving two Chicago men, Richard Loeb and Nathan Leopold, who in 1924 had murdered a young boy for no other reason than the thrill of it and the chance to prove they were "superior beings." In Hamilton's play, the two killers have strangled an acquaintance in their apartment and hidden the body in a trunk in their living room; they then hold a dinner party in which the victim's father is one of the guests. The play ends when their crime is exposed.

In planning the film, Hitchcock decided to turn *Rope* into one of the boldest technical experiments of his career. All the action in the original play took place on a single set over the course of an evening, and Hitchcock wanted to preserve this unity on film. He therefore decided to shoot the picture as a series of lengthy shots—some lasting nearly ten minutes and bridged, or connected, by primarily "hidden" cuts. Hitchcock disguised the cuts by ending one shot on a dark area that temporarily blacked out the screen. He then began the next shot exactly where the previous one had left off. As a result, the film seemed to unfold as a continuous action.

This method required planning even more meticulous than was usual for a Hitchcock film. The set was designed so that the walls and furniture could be moved quickly to make room for the camera, which roamed around throughout the course of the film, continually reframing the action. The lighting of the scenery outside the window, a painted cityscape, had to be carefully controlled to show the transition from late afternoon to night. The actors and crew were under particular pressure. If anyone made a mistake during one of the long shots, it had to be done over from the beginning. Also, *Rope* was Hitchcock's first film in color, and that too presented special problems. As shooting progressed, Hitchcock viewed the footage and saw that during moments when the sun was supposed to be setting, the color was all wrong—it was a much too garish orange. Several reels had to be reshot as a result.

Hitchcock later considered *Rope* an interesting failure at best. Its technique, he admitted, actually went against many of his ideas about "pure cinema," which to him had to include the tensions and rhythms produced by cutting, by placing one shot next to another in order to tell the story. "I undertook *Rope* as a stunt," the director said. "That's the only way I can describe it. I really don't know how I came to indulge in it."

Stunt or no, the film at least introduced Hitchcock to actor James Stewart, who had risen to major stardom before the war in such films as *Mr. Smith Goes to Washington* (1939) and *The Philadelphia Story* (1940). Military service had interrupted his career, but now he was making a comeback. His role in *Rope*, as an elitist philosophy professor who uncovers the murder, was part of an effort by the actor to shift from comic portrayals to more dramatic ones. He would achieve that goal with much help from Hitchcock: In the next decade they would make three more movies together. Only Cary Grant would hold a comparable place in Hitchcock's cinematic universe.

Rope received generally good reviews—along with publicity about its long-take techniques—and it managed to make a small profit. The same could not be said for the next production of Transatlantic Pictures, which was filmed in England during the late summer and early autumn of 1948.

Hitchcock arrived in London accompanied by Alma and Patricia. The couple's daughter, now 20, was still serious about an acting career, and she enrolled in the Royal Academy of Dramatic Art. Her father, meanwhile, went to work at the same studios where he had once made films for British International Pictures.

In some ways, *Under Capricorn* was a strange undertaking for Hitchcock. A costume drama set in 19th-century Australia, it had scarcely any thriller elements. The story concerned a well-born English lady unhappily married to a onetime convict and the complications that arise when her cousin arrives for a visit. Once again, miscasting was a problem. Although Hitchcock said he made the film because it suited Ingrid Bergman, the Swedish actress was an odd choice for the lead. Joseph Cotten, who had performed so brilliantly in *Shadow of a Doubt*, was also wrong in the part of the husband. As with Louis Jourdan in *The Paradine Case*, a rougher, less elegant actor was needed. Hitchcock admitted that an actor like Burt Lancaster might have been a better choice.

In shooting this rather stuffy melodrama, the director decided to continue the long-take experiments of *Rope*. There was no attempt to duplicate that film's illusion of unbroken time, but *Under Capricorn* would contain many lengthy shots, some quite elaborately staged. The requirements of this shooting method—a moving camera, moving walls and furniture, and long rehearsals with the actors—became too much for Bergman, who openly voiced her displeasure. She became so exhausted and bewildered at one point that she launched into a tirade on the set. Hitchcock, who hated arguments and confrontations of any sort, quietly slipped away. Later he learned that Bergman had continued to rant for 20 minutes without even noticing his absence.

By the next day, she had calmed down. "Okay, Hitch," she told him, "we'll do it your way."

"It's not my way, Ingrid," Hitchcock replied. "It's the *right* way!"

Like *Rope*, *Under Capricorn* was shot in color. That plus the lavish costumes and sets—not to mention Bergman's big-star salary—made for an expensive film. Costing $2.5 million, it opened in 1949 to negative reviews and poor business. Hitchcock later said that he felt uncomfortable making costume films because he knew so little about how people in other time periods behaved in their day-to-day lives. "If I had been thinking clearly," he told an interviewer in the 1960s, "I'd never have tackled a costume picture. You'll notice that I haven't done any since that time."

The failure of *Under Capricorn* sank Transatlantic Pictures and the Hitchcock-Bernstein partnership. Luckily, Hitchcock was able to reach an agreement with Warner Bros. in which he would act as a producer-director. Under this contract, he was to complete four films for a salary package totaling nearly $1 million. Aiding him in the negotiations for this deal was the giant MCA talent agency, which had been representing him since the mid–1940s, following the death of Myron Selznick. Lew Wasserman,

MCA's president, was by now one of Hitchcock's closest associates, and he would continue to play a key role in the director's career in the years ahead.

The first film to come from the Warners deal was *Stage Fright*, based on Selwyn Jepson's novel *Man Running*. What probably drew Hitchcock to the story was its theatrical background and the various sorts of role-playing and deception on which the plot turns. Its heroine is a young London drama student—just as Patricia Hitchcock was at the time—who assumes a false identity in her efforts to protect a man sought for murdering the husband of a famous actress. Yet what seems at first to be another of Hitchcock's "wrong man" movies holds a surprise twist: for once, the fugitive actually is guilty.

Like *Under Capricorn*, *Stage Fright* was shot in England. Accordingly, most of the cast were British performers— Richard Todd, Alastair Sim, Dame Sybil Thorndike— although the two leading female parts went to established Hollywood stars. Jane Wyman, who had just won an Oscar for her role as a deaf-mute girl in *Johnny Belinda* (1948), was cast as the drama student, while the German-born screen legend Marlene Dietrich, in the role of the famous actress, played what was basically a version of herself. Hitchcock also decided to enhance Patricia's practical experience by giving her a small role as one of Wyman's friends.

When *Stage Fright* was released early in 1950, neither critics nor audiences found it to be top-drawer Hitchcock; complaints about its "laggard rhythm," as the *New York Herald-Tribune* reviewer put it, were common. The movie's failure and the fact that Hitchcock could not find any suitable new projects caused him several months of anxiety. His worries began to ease only when he read a novel that spring by a first-time author. In Patricia Highsmith's *Strangers on a Train*, the director immediately saw the makings of his next film. In the novel, Highsmith told of two men who chance to meet on a cross-country rail journey. One is Guy Haines, a rising young architect; the other is a boozy, obviously psychopathic playboy named Bruno. Engaging Guy in conversation, Bruno proposes a bizarre scheme—an "exchange of murders." Bruno offers to kill the architect's unfaithful wife, freeing him to marry the woman he truly loves, if Guy will agree to murder Bruno's hated father. This plan will confound the police, Bruno argues, because no one will be able to connect the killers to their respective crimes or to each other. Though disturbed by the meeting, Guy puts it out of his head until Bruno actually murders his wife and then expects the architect to uphold his end of the "bargain." Eventually, under relentless pressure from Bruno, Guy does so. The playboy then dies in a boating accident, and Guy, consumed by guilt and self-hatred, is caught by a clever detective.

To script the film version, Hitchcock hired the famed mystery writer Raymond Chandler, creator of the private-eye character Philip Marlowe. Several of Chandler's own novels—notably *The Big Sleep*, *The Lady in the Lake*, and *Farewell, My Lovely*—had already been filmed, and Chandler had also written the screenplays for such movies as *Double Indemnity* (1944) and *The Blue Dahlia* (1946). On paper, a Chandler-Hitchcock collaboration may have looked like a grand alliance. It was anything but that.

Things were unpleasant from the start. Chandler hated Hitchcock's method of working closely with writers—what he called the "god-awful jabber sessions" in which ideas were freely exchanged and adopted or discarded. This practice, Chandler felt, cramped his style, although later he complained of the opposite problem, that Hitchcock was ignoring him. Moody and mercurial, Chandler would describe Hitchcock at one point as "as nice as can be"; at other times, he could barely disguise his contempt for the director.

It all became too much for Hitchcock. He disliked Chandler's drafts of the script and could not abide the writer's temperamental manner. Finally, he dismissed Chandler and hired Czenzi Ormonde, an assistant to Ben

Hecht, who completely rewrote the script. Alma also contributed to the final touches. Little of what Chandler had written remained in the finished film, although he still received a screen credit.

Not much of Highsmith's novel is left in the film, either. The early portions of the story—the exchange-of-murders proposal and Bruno's killing of Guy's wife—are still there since these were the elements that most appealed to Hitchcock. However—in part because of the Hollywood convention requiring a sympathetic hero—Guy refuses, in the film, to murder Bruno's father. Instead, toward the end, he openly defies Bruno, who in turn tries to frame Guy for the murder of his wife. In another departure from the book, Guy's profession was changed from architect to champion tennis player. This alteration allowed for the inclusion of an exciting sequence in which Guy's efforts to win a tennis match are intercut with Bruno's desperate attempts to retrieve a cigarette lighter that he plans to plant at the scene of the crime in order to implicate Guy.

Like *Shadow of a Doubt*, *Strangers on a Train* is a movie about "doubles." Bruno is clearly Guy's double—the man who carries out his dark wishes—and this pattern is extended to other characters and situations. Two detectives shadow Guy after he falls under suspicion for his wife's murder. Two female characters (one of them played by Patricia Hitchcock) wear eyeglasses. Two scenes occur in an amusement park. In the film's first dialogue scene, there are prominent reference to "doubles" in tennis, and Bruno orders two double-shot drinks.

Another important pattern in *Strangers* is "crisscross," the word Bruno uses to describe his chance meeting with Guy on the train and his deranged exchange-of-murders proposal. Appropriately, the film brims with crisscross imagery: intersecting train tracks, an engraving of crossed tennis racquets on Guy's cigarette lighter, the paths of ball and players on a tennis court. Thus, in purely visual ways, Hitchcock reinforces the idea that Guy and Bruno's destinies are intertwined, or crisscrossed. "Isn't it a fascinating design?" Hitchcock said of the film's form. "One could study it forever."

He was less happy with some of the casting decisions. Neither Farley Granger, as Guy, nor Ruth Roman, as the woman he hopes to marry, was much of an anchor for the audience's sympathies. Fortunately, for the role of Bruno, Hitchcock got exactly the actor he wanted—Robert Walker. A boyish charmer known mainly for romantic roles in such films as *Since You Went Away* (1944) and *The Clock* (1945), Walker was Hitchcock's most compelling psychopath since Joseph Cotten's Uncle Charlie. (Sadly, it turned out to be one of his last film appearances: Walker died, at age 32, only a year later.)

Released during the summer of 1951, *Strangers on a Train* enjoyed the success that had eluded *Under Capricorn* and *Stage Fright*. But then Hitchcock hit a dry spell that lasted several months. Searching for material on which to base his next movie, he read novel after novel; none of them seemed right. Developments on the home front may have preoccupied him. In January 1952, Patricia was married to Joseph E. O'Connell, a Massachusetts businessman whom she had met on a European vacation the previous spring. The marriage effectively ended her acting career, although as a favor to her father, she would return to the screen a few years later for a small role in *Psycho*.

Hitchcock's professional lull was finally broken when, at Alma's suggestion, he took a new look at a

The director offers advice to his daughter on the set of Strangers on a Train. *Patricia Hitchcock appears in three of her father's movies;* Stage Fright *(1950) and* Psycho *(1960) are the other two.*

property he had purchased several years earlier: a French play, first written in 1902, entitled *Nos deux consciences* ("Our two consciences"). The play spoke directly to Hitchcock's Catholicism and his familiarity with the church's traditions. It concerns a priest who hears a murderer's confession but cannot reveal what he knows—even after he himself is accused of the crime. Updating the story and renaming it *I Confess*, Hitchcock filmed it in Québec, Canada, during the autumn of 1952. With its strong French heritage, Québec was a city steeped in Catholicism, and its striking church architecture served Hitchcock well. His leading man, however, was another matter.

Playing the beleaguered priest was Montgomery Clift, a talented actor who was quite popular at the time. Unfortunately, Clift also had personal problems, notably alcoholism, that made him difficult to work with. Moreover, his approach to performance, while often brilliant in its results, ran against Hitchcock's grain. Trained in the so-called "method school" of acting, Clift wanted to find the proper motivation for every action his character took. When Hitchcock asked Clift to look upward at the end of a shot, the visual-minded director was thinking of how that shot would match with the one that would follow it on the screen. Clift, however, wanted to know why his character would look in that direction. Such clashes taxed Hitchcock's patience. Making matters worse was Clift's insistence that his acting coach be present on the set and that she approve his performance at every step.

Partly because of the tensions with Clift during filming, Hitchcock never regarded *I Confess* with much affection. He also felt that the movie lacked humor and that its core situation confused too many viewers: "We Catholics know that a priest cannot disclose the secret of the confessional, but the Protestants, the atheists, and the agnostics all say, 'Ridiculous! No man would remain silent and sacrifice his life for such a thing.'"

A tense moment in Dial "M" for Murder, *in which Grace Kelly receives a phone call intended to distract her from the killer (Anthony Dawson) hired by her husband.*

As *I Confess* was being released in February 1953, Hitchcock was busily searching for one last project to fulfill his obligations to Warner Bros. He decided on Frederick Knott's play *Dial "M" for Murder*, a hit on both the New York and London stages. In this melodrama, a devious husband hires a man to murder his wife, but the plan goes awry when she kills her attacker with a pair of scissors. The husband then makes it appear that the killing was not self-defense but murder. The wife is tried, found guilty, and sentenced to death. On the eve of her execution, a police inspector sympathetic to her plight uncovers the truth.

The cast included Ray Milland as the husband and, as the wife, a rising and beautiful young star named Grace Kelly. A former fashion model who had appeared in Fred Zinnemann's *High Noon* (1952) and John Ford's *Mogambo* (1953), Kelly enjoyed working for Hitchcock more than any of her previous directors. Hitchcock's cinematic expertise taught her, she said, "a tremendous amount about motion picture making"; plus, he boosted her self-confidence. For his part, Hitchcock found Kelly, with her cool, blonde elegance, ideally suited to his style—probably more so than any other actress he ever employed. He disdained the manner of stars like Marilyn Monroe, who flaunted their sexiness; he preferred performers like Kelly, who kept their passionate side under wraps and revealed it only at key moments.

Hitchcock got along so well with Kelly that some observers even speculated that he was infatuated with her. Whether that was true or not, it is clear that the director appreciated not only Kelly's beauty but also her sense of humor. As he sometimes did with people in order to disarm them, he one day told some off-color stories in her presence and asked her if she was shocked. "No," Kelly replied, "I went to a girl's convent school, Mr. Hitchcock; I heard all those things when I was 13." Her answer delighted the director.

If working with Kelly on *Dial "M" for Murder* was a pleasure for Hitchcock, the movie's technical side was an unpleasant chore. Studio head Jack Warner insisted that the movie be shot in the "3-D" process, which gave the images an illusion of depth. The process was then enjoying a brief surge of popularity, as movie companies scrambled to give audiences things they could not see on the new medium of television. The 3-D cameras were enormous and cumbersome, however, which made the process a burden for the filmmakers. It was a burden for the audience as well: Watching 3-D movies required wearing special glasses, which theater ushers had to hand out at the door.

By the time *Dial "M" for Murder* was released in the spring of 1954, the 3-D fad had passed, and as a result, few such prints of the film were even distributed. Most theaters showed the movie in regular two-dimensional format. This hardly detracted from its box-office appeal, for *Dial "M" for Murder* would prove to be a hit with audiences. Even greater success, however, would greet the director's next effort.

Hitchcock surveys the set during the filming of Rear Window. *The elaborate courtyard, representing a cluster of buildings in New York City's Greenwich Village, was constructed inside a huge soundstage at Paramount Pictures.*

CHAPTER

9

A NEW CONTRACT WITH PARAMOUNT

Even while *Dial "M" for Murder* was in production, the director was already looking ahead to his next picture. He had purchased rights to "Rear Window," a short story by the popular crime-fiction writer Cornell Woolrich; adapting it would be Hitchcock's first project for Paramount Pictures—the beginning of a new multipicture deal that Lew Wasserman had negotiated with the studio. James Stewart and Grace Kelly were signed for the leads. A young writer named John Michael Hayes, another MCA client, penned the screenplay. Filming took place during the winter of 1953–54.

Greatly expanding Woolrich's original story, the movie centered on a professional photographer named L. B. Jeffries (Stewart) who has broken his leg and is confined to a wheelchair in his New York apartment. Out of boredom, he becomes a voyeur, "peeping" on his neighbors across the courtyard. The mysterious goings-on in one apartment intrigue him, and eventually Jeffries is convinced that a murder has taken place there. He resolves to expose the killer, a salesman named Lars Thorwald (Raymond Burr), and in the process he puts both himself and his girlfriend, Lisa Fremont (Kelly), in grave danger.

HITCHCOCK ON DIRECTION

Hitchcock wrote a substantial portion of the entry on motion pictures in the 1965 edition of the Encyclopaedia Britannica. *In the following excerpts from that article, he offers his own description of what a film director does—or should do.*

Film direction was born when for the first time a man held a motion picture camera and turning it on his friend said, "Do something." This was the first step in creating movement for the camera. To create things that move for the camera is the aim at all times of the storytelling director.

Documentary direction is different. Its directors are primarily editors or, rather, discoverers. Their material is provided beforehand by God and man, noncinema man, man who is not doing things primarily for the camera. On the other hand, pure cinema has nothing in itself to do with actual movement. Show a man looking at something, say a baby. Then show him smiling. By placing these shots in sequence—man looking, object seen, reaction to object—the director characterizes the man as a kindly person. Retain shot one (the look) and shot three (the smile) and substitute for the baby a girl in a bathing costume, and the director has changed the characterization of the man. . . .

Motion pictures would be a source of much richer enjoyment, as is the case in other arts, if the audience were aware of what is and what is not well done. The mass audience has had no education in technique of cinema, as they frequently have in art and music, from their school days. They think only of story. The film goes by them too fast. The director, then, must be aware of this and must seek to remedy it. Without the audience being aware of what he is doing, he will use his technique to create an emotion in them. Suppose he is presenting a fight—the traditional fight in the barroom or elsewhere. If he puts the camera far enough back to take in the whole episode at once, the audience will follow at a distance, and objectively, but they will not really feel it. If the director moves his camera in and shows the details of the fight—flaying hands, rocking heads, dancing feet, put together in a montage of quick cuts—the effect will be totally different and the spectator will be writhing in his seat, as he would be at a real boxing match.

In *Lifeboat*, *Rope*, and much of *Dial "M" for Murder*, Hitchcock had worked within the limits of a single set. For *Rear Window* he took on that challenge again, but the single set in this instance proved to be quite an elaborate one—the most elaborate, in fact, ever built at Paramount up to that time. It included not only Jeffries's apartment but also the buildings surrounding the courtyard. Dotting the walls of those buildings were more than forty windows, some of them revealing fully furnished rooms. As the film unfolds, these windows also reveal a variety of "mini-dramas" that entertain both Jeffries and the audience. We see an attractive dancer practicing her movements, a lonely woman pining for love, a middle-aged couple doting over their dog, and a young songwriter struggling with his latest composition.

For this movie, Hitchcock made extensive use of what he called the "subjective technique." The term refers to a method of filming that tries to recreate a character's point of view by intercutting shots of the character looking at something with shots of what he sees. Hitchcock used this technique in virtually all his films but never more brilliantly than in *Rear Window*. Since the film's protagonist is constantly watching his neighbors, increasingly concentrating on the one who may have committed murder, the method was perfectly suited to the story. Seeing the events largely through Jeffries's eyes, we are compelled to identify with him and to experience the same feelings of curiosity, suspicion, and fear that he experiences.

The technique is especially effective in one suspenseful scene. Jeffries's girlfriend, Lisa, decides on her own to break into the suspected killer's apartment to search for an incriminating bit of evidence. Along with Jeffries, we gaze in horror as Lisa conducts her search while, unbeknownst to her, Thorwald approaches his door from the outside hallway. We see Thorwald accost Lisa in the apartment as the frantic Jeffries phones the police, who arrive just in time to save her. During the police questioning, Thorwald notices a signal

Lisa makes to Jeffries, still watching from across the courtyard, and suddenly the suspected killer spots the
man who has been spying on him. The entire sequence is
seen from Jeffrie's distanced vantage point: we hear only the
muffled sounds of voices in the encounter between
Thorwald and Lisa, but the scene is so expertly staged and
edited—so visual—that we have no trouble understanding
what is going on.

Entertaining from start to finish (and a huge hit with
audiences upon its release in August 1954), *Rear Window* is
typically ranked with Hitchcock's finest work. The overall
tone of Hayes's screenplay is light and witty, and the pairing
of Stewart and Kelly—ably supported by Thelma Ritter as
Stewart's funny and outspoken nurse—makes for an
extremely watchable cast. Underneath the lightness, however, lie some serious concerns.

The film's most important element is the romance
between Jeffries and Lisa. He resists committing himself to
their relationship and refuses to give her what she wants:
marriage. In both his job as a world-traveling photographer
and his new "hobby" of playing peeping Tom, he obviously
prefers observing other people's lives to putting his own life
in order. Although Lisa is devoted to him, Jeffries brims with
excuses about why they are not right for each other. He
shows more passion in his eagerness to prove Thorwald a
murderer than he does when he holds Lisa in his arms.

The murder that Jeffries uncovers mirrors, in a disturbing way, his situation with Lisa. At the beginning of the
movie, Thorwald is being nagged by his invalid wife.
Although Jeffries knows little about the particulars of the
Thorwald household, he assumes without a second thought
that the salesman wants to be rid of her. Thus, when the
wife does disappear, Jeffries immediately concludes that
Thorwald has murdered her. Would he assume this so readi-
ly if a romantic relationship of his own were not troubling
him? Jeffries's unconscious identification with Thorwald

recalls the "doubles" of *Shadow of a Doubt* and *Strangers on a Train*: once more, hero and villain are not so far apart.

Hitchcock's collaboration with John Michael Hayes on *Rear Window* went so well that the two would continue working together—and at a fast pace. Their next two projects, *To Catch a Thief* and *The Trouble with Harry*, were both filmed in 1954 and released the following year. Both films were comedies, and, though very different from each other, each was entertaining in its own way. Neither, however, matched the artistic achievement of *Rear Window*.

Set on the French Riviera, *To Catch a Thief* told the story of a retired jewel thief named John Robie, who

Cary Grant, standing in the warm waters of the Mediterranean, talks with the director during the filming of To Catch a Thief. *Wearing a robe and standing next to Hitchcock is Grace Kelly, who later became the Princess of Monaco, the tiny country near where the film was set.*

103

becomes romantically involved with Frances Stevens, a beautiful, wealthy American tourist. A sudden string of new thefts throws suspicion on Robie, and he enlists Frances's aid in helping him expose the real culprit. Cary Grant, working with Hitchcock for the first time since *Notorious*, made a perfect Robie, and Grace Kelly, as Frances, was as dazzling and elegant as ever. Light and frothy, *To Catch a Thief* was like a vacation for the director, who relished the opportunity it gave him to shoot its exterior scenes on location in southern France.

The Trouble with Harry took him to a very different location. The novel on which it was based was set in an English country village. Hitchcock decided to reset it in northern Vermont, and he scheduled the production for September, just as the leaves were changing color. Nature interfered with Hitchcock's well-laid plans, however. Heavy rain forced much of the shooting indoors, onto a set built inside a gymnasium. The crew was able to get no more than a few shots of the stunning New England foliage.

The autumnal background was meant to enhance the mood of the story, which revolved around a bothersome corpse. When the title character is found dead at the edge of town, various locals assume that someone has killed him, either by accident or by intent. No one is quite sure what to do with the corpse, and it keeps turning up at embarrassing moments. It is all very droll—and very English in its macabre humor—so it naturally appealed to Hitchcock.

The humor was perhaps too macabre for American audiences, and the film was a commercial dud. (*To Catch a Thief*, by contrast, was a big success.) Despite its failure, *The Trouble with Harry* remained a favorite of Hitchcock's. It launched the career of a major new star, Shirley MacLaine, who played Harry's young widow. It also marked Hitchcock's first film with composer Bernard Herrmann, whose memorable musical scores had enhanced movies ranging from *Citizen Kane* (1941) to *The Day the Earth Stood*

Still (1951). Herrmann became a regular member of the "Hitchcock team" that by now included a number of other talented collaborators: cinematographer Robert Burks, assistant director Herbert Coleman, editor George Tomasini, and costume designer Edith Head. Working with familiar people was important to Hitchcock, and their dedication in helping him achieve his goals was indispensable to his continued success.

Hitchcock had reached one of the busiest points in his career. Having completed four films in less than two years, he had his next project lined up as 1955 began. It would be a Hollywood version of his British classic *The Man Who Knew Too Much*. He believed that the main story elements—the plight of a couple suddenly enmeshed in international intrigue and confronted with the kidnapping of their child—would appeal strongly to American audiences, especially with American stars in the leads. Since the 1940s, in fact, he had considered remaking the movie. Now he believed the time was right, and in January, John Michael Hayes went to work on the screenplay.

With preparations underway for that production, the director attended to several other matters. That spring he finally decided, after 16 years in the United States, to become an American citizen. Alma and Patricia had already obtained citizenship, and Hitchcock could now admit to himself that the United States was their permanent home. After all, the failure of Transatlantic Pictures had squashed his dream of working in Britain on a regular basis, and as a producer-director in Hollywood, he was enjoying unprecedented artistic freedom. On April 20 he appeared at the Los Angeles County Courthouse for the swearing-in ceremony. Champagne, cake, and congratulations awaited him upon his return to the studio that day.

That same spring he reached a pair of agreements that would truly make his name a household word. First, he was approached by Richard Decker, a businessman who had an idea for a publishing venture he planned to call *The Alfred Hitchcock Mystery Magazine*. Decker simply obtained permission to use Hitchcock's name and thus capitalize on the director's reputation as the Master of Suspense. Otherwise, Hitchcock had nothing to do with the publication, which brought out a new collection of mystery stories each month. In the meantime, Lew Wasserman proposed a venture that would involve him more directly. The MCA head wanted Hitchcock to host a weekly television series to be called *Alfred Hitchcock Presents*. Recognizing the lucrative possibilities of TV, Hitchcock agreed. It was soon announced that the series would debut on the Columbia Broadcasting System (CBS) that fall.

By summer the planned remake of *The Man Who Knew Too Much* was ready for the cameras. In the role of the father, James Stewart signed on for his third Hitchcock film. His co-star was Doris Day, who was best known as a singer and musical comedy actress. Hitchcock had met Day a few years before at a party, where he told her how much he had liked her performance (her only "serious" one up to that time) in the melodrama *Storm Warning* (1951). They must work together sometime, the director had said. Day was flattered by the remark and somewhat surprised when, in 1955, Hitchcock finally made good on it.

The filming, however, was a challenge for the 31-year-old actress. Location work in London and the North African country of Morocco was required, and Day had never before been on an airplane or outside the United States. The poverty she saw in Morocco, not to mention the extreme heat and exotic food, troubled her considerably, but Hitchcock's manner on the set vexed her even more. He never spoke to her except to give her the most basic of instructions. She convinced herself that he hated her performance and regretted that he had ever cast her. Finally she summoned the courage to tell him that if he wanted to replace her, she would withdraw from the picture.

Hitchcock was genuinely surprised. He assured Day that her performance was perfect and that if she ever did anything *wrong*, he certainly would tell her.

Day's performance *is* excellent in *The Man Who Knew Too Much*. The question of how good the film is, however, has divided Hitchcock's fans, igniting a debate about whether it is better than the British original. The first version, filmed on a low budget with few technical resources at the director's disposal, makes up for its meager production values with its fast-paced action and funny dialogue. The second version is a far more elaborate production using exotic locales, lavish sets, color cinematography, and big-name stars. Despite its Hollywood polish, however, many have found this version plodding and stodgy, lacking the witty spontaneity of the original.

On the other hand, defenders of the American version find in it a depth of emotion lacking in the British film. There is a stronger emphasis on the relationship between the husband and wife, on the strains in their marriage, and on the ways they come to work together in order to recover their child. Much of the film's emotional impact rides on Day's performance, and she especially shines in two scenes. In the first of these, she learns of the kidnapping and then goes to pieces before our eyes, blighted with grief and near-hysteria, while her husband (a doctor in this version) tries to calm her with a dose of sedatives.

Day performs just as memorably in Hitchcock's restaging of the attempted assassination in the Royal Albert Hall. As usual, the director constructed the sequence with meticulous care, building suspense by brilliantly juggling its various elements: the orchestra and chorus, the assassin and his target, and the distraught mother. But more than anything, the repeated shots of Day—marvelously conveying the distress of a woman torn between her desire to thwart the assassination and her knowledge that doing so may cost the life of her child—are what anchor the scene and make it work.

Wacky props, like these sausages wrapped around the portly film-maker's belly, added to the comic tone of Hitchcock's appearances as host of a weekly television series during the 1950s and 1960s. The popular show lasted for 10 seasons.

Unfortunately, *The Man Who Knew Too Much* marked the souring of the director's relations with John Michael Hayes. Having written four screenplays for Hitchcock, Hayes felt that his payment for all that work, a total of only $75,000, was too low. Hayes became even more distressed when Hitchcock insisted that Angus MacPhail, an old friend from England, be given credit, along with Hayes, for the screenplay of *The Man Who Knew Too Much*. MacPhail had joined the production as a consultant, but according to Hayes, he was by then "a dying alcoholic" who made no real contribution to the script. Hayes took the matter to the Screen Writers Guild, which agreed that Hayes should receive sole credit. This dispute ended what had otherwise been one of the smoothest series of collaborations in Hitchcock's career.

Meanwhile, the debut that autumn of *Alfred Hitchcock Presents* began bringing the filmmaker into millions of American homes on a weekly basis. The show made his double-chinned visage as famous as the faces of any of his glamorous stars. The show ran in a half-hour format from 1955–62. In the fall of 1962, it became *The Alfred Hitchcock Hour* and was finally retired in 1965. Over the course of the show's 10-season history, Hitchcock himself directed 20 episodes. His main job, however, was to appear at the beginning and end of each episode, delivering a whimsical monologue, in which he usually poked fun at the show's commercial sponsors. Amusing props—such as a fake arrow through the director's head—were often used to add to the jokey atmosphere. The show's theme music was a snippet from Charles François Gounod's "Funeral March of a Marionette," which became forever associated with Hitchcock, as did his opening greeting of "Good eev-e-ning," drawled in a distinctive voice that still bore the accent of his native England.

The TV show reunited Hitchcock professionally with Joan Harrison, his onetime assistant. Hired as a producer for the series, Harrison made sure that the tone of the televised stories properly reflected the mix of suspense and humor that audiences enjoyed in Hitchcock's big-screen work. And each week it was a brand new story with a different cast— what was known in the television trade as an "anthology format." The constant factor in the series, in addition to Hitchcock's appearance as host, was the surprise twist that ended each show.

The premiere episode, "Revenge," which aired on October 2, 1955, was directed by Hitchcock. The story involved a woman who tells her husband that she has been attacked. When she later identifies someone as the assailant, the husband goes after the man and kills him. At the end of the story, the wife suddenly identifies another man as the attacker. The husband, to his horror, realizes that his wife is delusional, that the original attack never occurred, and that he has murdered someone for nothing.

Playing the disturbed wife in "Revenge" was a young actress named Vera Miles. Hitchcock saw in her the makings of a new star, which at that moment he desperately needed. That same year, to his chagrin, Grace Kelly decided to retire from the ranks of Hollywood royalty to become real royalty. She announced her engagement to Prince Rainier of Monaco, a tiny country on the Riviera close to where many of the locations for *To Catch a Thief* had been filmed. Kelly and Rainier would marry the following spring. Losing his ideal star put Hitchcock in search of a new one. He thought that Miles might have that potential.

He soon cast her in his next film, which would differ sharply from the movies that preceded it. Warner Bros. owned a film treatment based on a *Life* magazine article that had appeared in 1953, and for a percentage of the potential profits Hitchcock agreed to direct it. Although he was still under contract to Paramount, the arrangement was non-exclusive, allowing him to make films for other studios.

Unlike the novels and short stories on which he usually based his films, this story was true. It concerned a New York musician named Christopher Emanuel Balestrero who had been arrested and brought to trial for a series of robberies. Falsely accused, Balestrero was finally cleared when another man, who closely resembled him, was caught and confessed to the crimes. The case was a real-life illustration of a favorite Hitchcock theme, one that the title of the movie perfectly expressed: *The Wrong Man*. Filming took place from March through May of 1956.

In its look and tone, *The Wrong Man* was nothing like the glossy, colorful features Hitchcock had been making for Paramount. Working from a script by Angus MacPhail and Maxwell Anderson (a Pulitzer Prize–winning playwright best known for such dramas as *Both Your Houses* and *Winterset*), Hitchcock went for a starker, more realistic approach. Starring Henry Fonda as Balestrero and Miles as his wife, Rose, the film was shot in black and white using many of the New York City locations where the actual events had occurred. Hitchcock's oft-confessed fear of the police fills the early scenes as Balestrero endures a nightmare of arrest and incarceration.

The tone grows even bleaker in the film's second half. Rose Balestrero gives in to the strain of the ordeal, suffering a nervous breakdown. Even when "the right man" is caught, she takes no comfort from it. In the last scene, Balestrero visits her at a psychiatric rest home where she seems hopelessly mired in depression. A final printed message, superimposed on the screen, tells us that Mrs.

Balestrero eventually made a full recovery, but this news hardly dispels the dark mood of the film.

Given that dark mood, it was probably no surprise that the film failed commercially upon its release in December 1956. Hitchcock himself claimed to be dissatisfied with *The Wrong Man*. He felt that in his effort to remain true to the facts, he had let the story veer away from Balestrero's dilemma to that of his wife. "It's possible," he said, "I was too concerned with veracity to take sufficient dramatic license."

Despite the occasional flop, like *The Wrong Man* or *The Trouble with Harry*, Hitchcock was functioning quite well in what some were calling the "New Hollywood." When he came to work in America in 1939, the studio system—with its factory-like style of production—was at its peak. A decade and a half later, that system had largely fallen apart. The reasons for its demise were complex and included such factors as the rise of television, a general decline in movie attendance, and government antitrust action that had forced the major studios to sell off their theater chains. Faced with such challenges, the movie companies found it increasingly cost-effective to lease their facilities to independent producers and to act as film distributors rather than as film "manufacturers."

Hitchcock's past experience had prepared him well for this new environment. His years of being loaned out by David Selznick had given him broad experience at a variety of studios, working under different executives. When, by the late 1940s, he had become his own producer, it was no problem for him to adapt to a world in which independents were becoming the norm rather than the exception. Moreover, aided by his weekly exposure on TV, he was now almost an industry unto himself—a brand name as familiar as "Chevrolet" or "General Electric." He had gained unprecedented artistic control, and he was about to make three of the best movies in his career.

In this publicity shot for Vertigo, *James Stewart and Kim Novak reenact the film's final scene. This exact image does not appear in the movie; rather, a still photographer posed it on the set for use in promoting the film.*

THREE
MASTERPIECES

As he awaited the release of *The Wrong Man*, Hitchcock weighed possibilities for his next picture at Paramount. The company owned rights to two novels that looked promising. One, Laurens van der Post's *Flamingo Feather*, was a spy thriller set in Africa. Hitchcock abandoned that project, however, after he visited South Africa, the planned location for the shooting, and met with government officials who showed little interest in cooperating with an American film company. This was just as well, since the other novel, *D'entre les morts* ("From Among the Dead") by the French writers Thomas Narcejac and Pierre Boileau, intrigued him much more.

An earlier book by the same authors had inspired a hit French thriller, *Les diaboliques* ("The Fiends"), directed by Henri-Georges Clouzot and released in America in 1955. Hitchcock hoped that his film of *D'entre les morts* might repeat that success. In Hitchcock's hands, the rather contrived mystery novel would be transformed into *Vertigo*. While its initial performance at the box office would prove disappointing, the film would endure as what many consider to be the director's supreme masterpiece.

Getting it to the screen, however, was itself a story with a few twists and turns. Casting the male lead was easy—James Stewart was perfect for the part—but the female lead presented some problems. Hitchcock originally wanted Vera Miles for the role, hoping she would indeed become the next Grace Kelly. That dream dissipated when the actress, who had recently married, became pregnant. Kim Novak, a performer with bigger name recognition than Miles, replaced her.

The screenplay stirred up even more anxiety than the casting. Fresh from writing *The Wrong Man*, Maxwell Anderson began work on the first draft in June 1956. When it became clear that Anderson's plotting and dialogue were just not working, Hitchcock again let his old chum Angus MacPhail give it a try. MacPhail, however, was still battling alcoholism and soon withdrew from the project. Another writer, Alec Coppel, improved on Anderson's efforts, but Hitchcock remained dissatisfied. Finally, Samuel Taylor, author of the play *Sabrina Fair*, took over, and he was able to breathe life into the characters and the story. In September 1957, 15 months after the process had begun, the screenplay—credited to both Coppel and Taylor—was ready.

It might have been finished sooner if Hitchcock's health had not caused additional delays. The director underwent minor surgery for a hernia and colitis (an inflammation of the colon) in January 1957, around the time Taylor was hired. Two months later, he suffered a much more serious problem involving his gallbladder. Timely surgery saved his life. As Hitchcock always worked closely with screenwriters, his hospitalization and recovery inevitably slowed down the preparations.

Once the script was completed, however, filming went smoothly—first in San Francisco, where the exterior scenes were shot, and then at the Paramount studios in Hollywood, where the interior work was done. In April 1958, however, as Hitchcock was putting the finishing touches on the film, another health crisis in his household added to the pressure. This time it was Alma who was affected; she was diagnosed with cervical cancer, and required surgery. The possibility of losing his life's companion terrified Hitchcock, but luckily, Alma recovered.

Vertigo was finally released in late May. What audiences saw was perhaps the strangest, yet most hauntingly beautiful film Hitchcock had ever made. At the time, its far-fetched plot drew a mixed response from critics—*Time* magazine sneeringly called the movie a "Hitchcock and bull story"— but today most agree that it is one of the director's most deeply felt pictures.

In *Vertigo*, a San Francisco police detective, John "Scottie" Ferguson (Stewart), resigns from the force when his fear of heights, or acrophobia, leads to the death of a fellow police-man during a rooftop chase. Afterward, an old friend, Gavin Elster (Tom Helmore), calls on him for a strange favor: He asks the ex-detective to follow his wife, Madeleine (Novak), who may be in danger. Scottie learns that Madeleine is appar-ently "possessed" by the spirit of her great-grandmother, who had tragically killed herself. Trailing Madeleine, Scottie sees some strange behavior. As if in a trance, she visits the grave of her forebear and sits before the woman's portrait at a museum. One day she tries to drown herself. Scottie, who has fallen in love with Madeleine, rescues her and vows to keep her safe. But his acrophobia again thwarts him: he cannot follow Madeleine to the top of a church tower, where she leaps to her death. Overcome with grief and guilt, Scottie spends a year in a mental institution.

After his release, he continues to obsess about Madeleine. One day he spots a young woman, Judy Barton (also played by Novak), who bears a striking resemblance to his lost love. He begins a strange courtship, attempting to remake Judy into the image of Madeleine. What he does not know, however, is that Judy really is "Madeleine." She had been part of an elaborate plot by Elster, her former lover, to murder his real wife and make it appear to be a suicide. At the film's finale, Scottie dis-covers the truth, drags Judy to the top of the tower where the murder took place, and forces her to confess. He overcomes his acrophobia, but Judy accidentally falls. Stunned and devastated, the hero stands at the edge of the tower, gazing down at the body of the woman who is now truly lost to him forever.

Hitchcock said that what appealed to him about the Narcejac–Boileau novel was "the hero's attempts to re-create the image of a dead woman through another who's alive." Indeed, the film becomes most troubling in its last third when Scottie buys Judy a Madeleine-style wardrobe and bullies her into dyeing her hair blonde to match Madeleine's. He cannot love Judy for who she is; he can only love his memory of Madeleine. His romantic obsession has him teetering at the edge of madness.

His situation is made even more disturbing by the fact that we know what Scottie does not know—that Judy is the same woman, that the "Madeleine" with whom he fell in love was a fake. In a bold move, Hitchcock and Taylor decided to reveal this plot twist to the audience right after Scottie first meets Judy. Thus, as we watch the final scenes, we are held in suspense, wondering how Scottie will react when he discovers the truth. More important, we realize that Scottie is focusing his obsession on someone who was never real in the first place. Our feelings are complicated further by our knowledge that Judy actually loves Scottie and submits to the makeover only to win his affection. However, by this time we also know that Scottie's delusions and Judy's guilt—her role in the murder plot—have already doomed that love.

Many elements came together to help turn *Vertigo* into the unforgettable film that it is: compelling performances by the two leads, a lush, romantic score by Bernard Herrmann, and beautiful use of locations in and around San Francisco. It was Hitchcock's masterful control of such elements, all orchestrated to create a dreamlike atmosphere and stir powerful emotions, that made the film a triumph of both style and substance.

Although *Vertigo* would not be properly appreciated for years, the director's next production would prove an instant crowd-pleaser. The making of *North by Northwest* took Hitchcock for the first and only time to the studios of Metro-Goldwyn-Mayer. As he had done with *The Wrong Man*, he exercised the non-exclusive clause in his contract with Paramount in order to make the picture. Interestingly, though, *North by Northwest* was not the film he had originally agreed to direct for MGM.

That picture was supposed to have been an adaptation of Hammond Innes's novel *The Wreck of the Mary Deare*, to which MGM owned film rights. As Hitchcock and screen-writer Ernest Lehman soon realized, however, the book had an intriguing opening—a ghost ship is found adrift in the middle of the English Channel—but an otherwise tedious plot. Neither man could figure out a way to make it work on film, so they decided to do something altogether different. As Lehman put it, they set out to make "the Hitchcock movie to end all Hitchcock movies."

North by Northwest was a return to the territory of *The 39 Steps*. Like the British classic, it focuses on an ordinary man who is caught in a spy plot, falsely accused of murder, and forced to run for his life. Along the way he finds romance and endures hair-raising adventures. Although Hitchcock reportedly approached James Stewart about the part, he really knew from the beginning that it was better suited to Cary Grant, his other favorite leading man. Grant, now in his mid-50s, was as suave and handsome as ever—so much so that no one thought any-thing of it when Hitchcock cast Jessie Royce Landis, an actress born in the same year as Grant, as the character's mother.

After the seriousness of *The Wrong Man* and *Vertigo*, *North by Northwest* was a lighthearted change of pace, a return to the sort of Hitchcock film many moviegoers expected. Filled with witty dialogue and amusing situations, the story took the viewer on a wild and delightful ride from one pic-turesque locale to another—from New York to Chicago to the Black Hills of South Dakota. It contained what is proba-bly the director's most famous action sequence, one in which

This poster for North by Northwest *depicts one of the surprising twists in the film's plot: the apparent shooting of Cary Grant by his costar Eva Marie Saint. The poster also uses Hitchcock's name as a selling point by placing it above the title—a form of billing that was granted to only a few top directors.*

Grant's character, an advertising executive completely out of his element, is terrorized in an open field by a small plane. Later, in a finale almost as exciting, the hero and heroine flee their pursuers by climbing down the giant stone faces of Mount Rushmore.

As in *Rear Window*, the light touch that makes *North by Northwest* so entertaining disguises deeper concerns. The illusion-versus-reality and false-identity themes that figure so strongly in *Vertigo* are here as well. Grant's character, Roger Thornhill, first becomes entangled in the spy plot when the spies mistake him for an American agent named George Kaplan. We soon learn that Kaplan does not even exist: He is a phantom decoy set up by U.S. intelligence to divert attention away from the real agent, Eve Kendall (Eva Marie Saint). The whole Kaplan charade underlines the superficiality of Thornhill's own personality. A glib ad man who tries at one point to wriggle out of his situation by declaring that he has "a job, a secretary, a mother, two ex-wives, and several bartenders dependent on me," Thornhill is a man who shuns commitment and revels in his own cynicism. Over the course of his adventures as "George Kaplan," however, he becomes a better man, falling in love with Eve (who is also not what she seems) and learning to trust her.

Costing $4.3 million, *North by Northwest* was Hitchcock's most expensive film since *The Paradine Case*, which had been a gigantic failure. This time, however, the lavish production paid off: the film earned $6 million following its July 1959 release. Having fulfilled his single-movie deal with MGM, Hitchcock still owed Paramount one last picture.

He originally intended to make *No Bail for the Judge*, based on an English novel about a woman lawyer who must defend her father on charges of murder. A major star, Audrey Hepburn, agreed to play the lead. Although Hitchcock usually favored blonde actresses, Hepburn was one brunette with an elegance that matched Grace Kelly's. But her collaboration with Hitchcock was not to be. Just as Vera Miles had done with *Vertigo*, Hepburn withdrew from the project when she became pregnant. Furious at this turn of events—as if Hepburn's pregnancy were somehow a personal betrayal—Hitchcock lost interest in the film and quickly put another project into motion.

Always a keen observer of box-office trends, the filmmaker had recently noticed how successful a number of low-budget horror movies had become, especially with young audiences. American-International Pictures, for example, had made small fortunes from such fare as *I Was a Teen-age Frankenstein* and *I Was a Teen-age Werewolf*, both released in 1957. Meanwhile, an independent producer-director named William Castle was enjoying similar success with a string of shockers, including *Macabre* (1958) and *The Tingler* (1959). Such movies were usually silly and poorly crafted. Hitchcock wondered how a cheaply made horror film might turn out with a master director in charge. That, he believed, would be an interesting challenge.

The source material he chose was Robert Bloch's recent novel *Psycho*. Bloch was a prolific spinner of horror yarns who had also written scripts for *Alfred Hitchcock Presents*. His book had been inspired by the grisly exploits of a midwestern serial killer named Ed Gein, and while its details were much less gruesome than those of the actual Gein case, it still contained some bloody shocks for the reader. Barely 25 pages into the novel, one character—an attractive young woman—steps into a motel shower and is murdered moments later by a knife-wielding maniac.

"I think the thing that appealed to me and made me decide to do the picture," Hitchcock said, "was the suddenness of the murder in the shower, coming, as it were, out of the blue." This was unusual for Hitchcock, who usually favored suspense over surprise. But of course he would be sure to pack *Psycho* with plenty of suspense as well.

Before he could start production, however, he hit a snag. Paramount executives thought the story was too lurid

HITCHCOCK ON ACTORS

Extracted from one of Hitchcock's after-dinner speeches, the following remarks were obviously played for laughs, but they also suggest why Hitchcock was never considered an "actor's director." For him, the actor's performance was but one element—though a crucial one, to be sure—in the overall design of a film. Also, his joke about the airplane from North by Northwest *hints at the resentment he often felt about the soaring salaries of star performers.*

There is a dreadful story that I hate actors. . . . I can't imagine how such a rumor began. Of course it may possibly be because I was once quoted as saying that actors are cattle. My actor friends know that I would never be capable of such a thoughtless, rude, and unfeeling remark; that I would never call them cattle. . . . What I probably said was that actors should be *treated* like cattle.

I will admit that I have, from time to time, hoped that technology would devise a machine that would replace the actor. And I have made some progress of my own in that direction. In *Foreign Correspondent* Joel McCrea played a scene with a windmill and in *North by Northwest* Cary Grant's *vis-a-vis* was a crop-dusting airplane. I believe the airplane had real star quality, for it drew an amazing amount of fan mail. However, when I attempted to sign it up for my next picture, it was already asking too much money.

This leads to the next logical step when I reduced the human element still further in *The Birds*. Now *there* are some actors I would call cattle! You have heard of actors who have insisted that their names be above the title; these demanded that they *be* the title! As a result I am definitely in favor of human actors. As far as I am concerned birds are "strictly for the birds"—or for Walt Disney.

and balked at financing it. Hitchcock responded with a counter-proposal. He would make the film with his own money, using the crew from his television show and filming it at the Universal studios, where the weekly TV episodes were shot. And like the TV show, it would be made in black and white on inexpensive sets. Paramount would only have to market and distribute it. Hitchcock even agreed to go without salary in exchange for 60 percent ownership of the film. Feeling they had little to lose, the Paramount bosses gave *Psycho* their approval.

For the screenplay, Hitchcock's agents at MCA pointed him to another of their clients, a former songwriter named Joseph Stefano. The young man's credits included only one other movie, *The Black Orchid* (1959), which Hitchcock disliked. Reluctantly, the director agreed to meet Stefano, and to his surprise, the two of them hit it off. "He found that I was very funny," Stefano recalled, "and we had a lot of laughs together."

Keeping one's sense of humor, Hitchcock felt, was essential in dealing with a book like *Psycho*. The main character, Norman Bates, is a pudgy, 40-year-old motel owner who is totally dominated by his tyrannical mother. Quickly we learn, or think we learn, that Mrs. Bates is a psychotic monster. She brutally murders a motel guest (the woman in the shower) because Norman is attracted to her. As a devoted son, Norman covers up his mother's crime and disposes of the body in a nearby swamp. Unbeknownst to Norman, however, the victim had earlier stolen $40,000 from her employer, and three people—her sister, an insurance detective, and her boyfriend—soon come looking for her. The detective is also killed, but the sister and boyfriend finally succeed in subduing and unmasking the murderous mother. As it turns out, "Mrs. Bates" is really Norman. Years before, we discover, Norman had killed his real mother, and unhinged by his deed, he often assumed her identity in an insane, guilt-ridden effort to convince himself that she was still alive.

Stefano was eager to work with Hitchcock, but he was less excited about the novel they were trying to adapt. He told the director that he "really didn't like this man, Norman Bates." However, when they began to discuss ways in which the novel could be altered for the screen, Stefano's imagination fired up.

Hitchcock wanted Stefano to stay close to Bloch's plot, but he agreed with the writer that the main character should be more sympathetic. Instead of hiring a plump, middle-aged actor for the part, Hitchcock suggested, why not make Norman into an attractive yet vulnerable young man? He knew of an actor—27-year-old Anthony Perkins—who had projected just those qualities in such films as *Friendly Persuasion* (1955) and *Fear Strikes Out* (1957). Luckily, Perkins was not only available but available at little cost: He owed Paramount a picture on his contract, and appearing in *Psycho* would fulfill his obligations to the studio.

Bloch's novel begins with Norman. Stefano wanted to open the film with the female character, showing why she steals the money and how she ends up at the Bates Motel. Hitchcock had an additional idea. He said they should cast a star in the role, an actress whom no one would expect to see killed only a third of the way into the picture. Janet Leigh, a popular performer who had been working in Hollywood for more than a decade, was chosen to play the victim, Marion Crane. Vera Miles, still under contract to Hitchcock, was picked for the role of Marion's sister, while John Gavin and Martin Balsam won the respective roles of boyfriend and detective. Patricia Hitchcock, as a favor to her father, took the small part of Leigh's office mate.

Hitchcock began shooting *Psycho* on November 30, 1959, and completed principal photography in 45 working days. Of all the scenes in the film, the one on which he spent the most time—an entire week—was the now-famous shower murder. Although it would last less than a minute on screen, the sequence required dozens of shots—of the shower head,

Hitchcock coaches Janet Leigh for the notorious shower scene in Psycho. *The sequence, which consumed barely a minute of screen time, took a week to film.*

of Leigh screaming, of a shadowy killer with a plunging knife, of blood (actually chocolate syrup) swirling into the drain beneath the victim's bare legs. The camera angles were so carefully chosen and the shots were edited together with such precision and rapidity that the scene seems more violent than it really is. In only one shot does the audience ever see the knife touch the actress's body, and that shot is bloodless. Adding to the impression of violence was Bernard Herrmann's music, which, for this scene, consisted of a series of violin "shrieks."

In later years a controversy arose about the shower scene. Saul Bass, a gifted graphic artist who designed the opening credits for the film, also prepared the storyboards for the shower sequence after Hitchcock told him about the kinds of shots he wanted. Later Bass suggested that he had actually directed the scene. Others who were there, notably Janet Leigh, have dismissed this claim. "I was in that shower for seven days," Leigh asserted, "and, believe you me, Alfred Hitchcock was right next to his camera for every one of those seventy-odd shots."

Whatever the truth about the shower scene, there is no question that *Psycho* had an enormous impact on audiences when it was released during the summer of 1960. Costing only $800,000, the movie became the biggest money-maker of Hitchcock's career. In its initial release, it generated $9 million in revenues. Many of the reviews were negative, but the public did not care. To this day, *Psycho* is still the first movie most people think of when they hear the director's name.

Hitchcock had accomplished what he set out to do. He had made a low-budget horror picture with great skill. But if *Psycho* were only a horror movie, it is doubtful that it would be so well remembered. As with the best of Hitchcock's work, the film not only rivets the viewer's attention, playing expertly on common fears and anxieties, it also succeeds as a work of art. *Psycho* is Hitchcock's most relentless journey into the darkness of the human soul, and the audience is carried along for every step of that journey.

The film begins with a desperate woman and an act of theft, and through a combination of Stefano's effective writing, Janet Leigh's sympathetic performance, and Hitchcock's subjective cinematic techniques, the audience is made to identify with her. When a policeman momentarily detains Marion, we want her to get away. When she imagines the reactions to her crime (heard in voice-over), we experience her fear and feelings of guilt. In a way, the film implicates us in the crime Marion has committed.

Once Marion is gone, we can only identify with Norman. Isolated and lonely, dominated by a tyrannical mother, he elicits our sympathy just as Marion did. We watch him cover up his mother's crime and want him to succeed. After he pushes Marion's car into the swamp, with her body in the trunk, we wait nervously with him as it starts to sink. For a moment it stops, and we gasp. Finally, the car disappears beneath the water, and we sigh in relief. With each twist in the story, Hitchcock exposes us to increasingly abnormal human behavior and makes us identify with it. We may not be as mad as Norman Bates, *Psycho* says, but none of us is innocent of the evil impulses it exposes.

In interviews, Hitchcock liked to describe *Psycho* as a "fun picture," akin to visiting the haunted house at an amusement park. Clearly it works on that level, but just as clearly it resonates on a much deeper one.

A large crowd gathers for the opening of The Birds *on Broadway in New York City. For weeks prior to the release of the film, the studio's promotional campaign teased the film-going public with the seemingly ungrammatical advertising line "The Birds Is Coming!"*

II

A NEW HOME AT UNIVERSAL

Early in 1962, Hitchcock settled into a new professional home: Universal Pictures, which had recently been purchased by MCA, the company that had represented him for years. In exchange for the rights to *Psycho* and his television series, he received a large chunk of MCA stock—becoming the company's third-largest shareholder, in fact—and a set of luxurious offices for himself and his staff. For the remainder of his career, his films would be released through Universal.

Coming off the big success of *Psycho*, he was now facing the question of what he could do to top it. Several potential projects fizzled before he turned to a property he had owned for years; it was a short story by Daphne du Maurier, the author of *Jamaica Inn* and *Rebecca*. Entitled "The Birds," the story concerned a series of unexplained bird attacks on people in a small English village. Hitchcock had all but forgotten about it when news items about real-life bird attacks in California caught his attention. Suddenly the idea of nature inexplicably turning on humanity appealed to him and clinched his decision. *The Birds* would be his next film.

Hitchcock first invited Joseph Stefano to write the screenplay, but Stefano could muster no enthusiasm for the project and politely declined. Eventually the director found the right scenarist in Evan Hunter, a popular and prolific novelist. Since there was little plot or character development in du Maurier's original story, Hunter and Hitchcock had to create the film's narrative almost from scratch. Only the mysterious bird attacks—the key plot element—would remain.

The Hitchcock/Hunter version of *The Birds* begins when a wealthy socialite named Melanie Daniels meets lawyer Mitch Brenner in San Francisco. When she travels to his seaside hometown of Bodega Bay, north of San Francisco, for a surprise visit, a seagull swoops down and cuts her forehead. Over the next two days, as a romance blossoms between Melanie and Mitch, the bird attacks escalate. A flock of sparrows invades the lawyer's living room; more seagulls attack children at a party; and a neighboring farmer is found dead—with his eyes pecked out. These incidents are followed by an attack on schoolchildren and on the town itself. Finally Melanie and Mitch, together with his family (consisting of his mother and young sister), barricade themselves in the Brenner home for yet another onslaught. After a brief lull, Melanie is trapped in the attic, where she is attacked by birds and badly injured. As the film ends, the small group, surrounded by hundreds of birds (now mysteriously quiet), pile into a car and drive off in search of medical attention for Melanie.

Hitchcock knew from the start that *The Birds* would be a costly production requiring elaborate camera trickery. To help save money, he cast the film with lesser-known performers who could be paid smaller salaries than big stars like James Stewart and Cary Grant. Australian-born actor Rod Taylor was cast as Mitch; Jessica Tandy, an acclaimed stage actress, was cast as his mother. For the role of Melanie Daniels, Hitchcock decided to gamble on a 26-year-old New York fashion model whose only previous acting experience had been in television commercials. In fact, it was in a commercial for a diet drink that Hitchcock first spotted the fresh-faced, blonde Tippi Hedren. He arranged to have her brought to

Hollywood for screen tests and soon announced that she would appear in *The Birds*.

As expected, the filming was fraught with challenges. The hundreds of special effects—some using mechanical birds, some using trick photography, and some using hordes of real birds—made it the director's most technically ambitious film. Of all the difficult scenes to shoot, none was more harrowing than the final attack on Melanie in the attic. In its use of quick cuts and dozens of angles to depict a woman under assault in a tight space, the scene was similar to the *Psycho* shower murder, but it proved far more difficult to film. Originally, Hitchcock's technicians planned to use mechanical birds. Unfortunately, their phoniness was all too obvious, and real crows and seagulls were substituted at the last minute.

So began what Hedren called "the worst week of my life." Off-camera, crew members hurled birds at her to give Hitchcock the shots he wanted. Shooting was constantly interrupted as make-up artists applied fake blood to Hedren's face, arms, and ankles. Wardrobe personnel tore her dress and stockings. Hedren's terrified reactions, as she endured take after take, became actual terror. Finally, the beak of one of the birds tore her lower eyelid. At this point she suffered a nervous collapse and had to be put under a doctor's care for several days. Hitchcock halted filming until she could return to the set.

According to Hedren, filming the scene distressed the director as well as herself. "Every time Hitch would say 'Cut,'" she recalled, "he was back in his office on the set and immediately closed the door. . . . I think he literally felt very guilty about what he had been putting me through."

So complicated was the production that *The Birds* required 20 weeks of filming during the spring and early summer of 1962, followed by several months of editing and special-effects work. When it was finally released in March 1963, it made a modest profit and met with a mixed response from critics. Many audiences and reviewers felt the film was

Tippi Hedren during the filming of the last bird attack in The Birds. *The shooting of this scene proved to be almost as harrowing to the actress as an actual attack would have been.*

implausible and were puzzled, even angered, by its inconclusive ending, which gives no hint of why the birds have been attacking or of what ultimately happens to the characters.

Yet what some saw as weaknesses, others have seen as strengths. *The Birds* has remained a favorite among many of Hitchcock's admirers. Indeed, it is probably the director's purest statement about the fragility of the civilized order and its vulnerability to chaos. That the birds and their destructive behavior cannot be explained seems to be Hitchcock's very point: Rationality ultimately fails when confronted with the disorder of the universe. The final, chilling image in the film—a tiny car receding into the distance amid a landscape crowded with birds—suggests the precariousness of human existence and the puniness of human responses to the irrational.

As *The Birds* was opening in theaters, Hitchcock and Evan Hunter were deep into preparations for Hitchcock's next film, *Marnie*. Following the premise of the Winston Graham novel on which it was based, the film would focus on a compulsive thief named Marnie Edgar, an attractive young woman whose problems can be traced back to a childhood trauma involving her man-hating mother, a former prostitute. When Mark Rutland, one of the employers she has stolen from, catches her, he vows to "cure" her and blackmails her into marrying him. She is sexually frigid, however, and refuses his advances. Finally—and here Hitchcock made one of his most daring decisions—the frustrated Rutland forces himself upon her, causing her later to attempt suicide. This scene caused Hitchcock and Hunter to part ways. The writer felt that the apparent rape, even discreetly handled, would alienate the audience. As he pleaded in a note to Hitchcock, "Mark is *not* that kind of person."

Hitchcock disagreed, however, feeling that the scene was essential to the movement of the plot. He found a new writer—the female playwright Jay Presson Allen, who would soon enjoy a stage success with her adaptation of Muriel Spark's novel *The Prime of Miss Jean Brodie*. Sensitive material like the *Marnie* script, Hitchcock thought, needed a woman's touch.

For the title role, Hitchcock had at first approached Princess Grace, hoping that it would mark her Hollywood comeback. When the citizens of Monaco learned of these plans, however, they understandably raised a fuss. Having their princess play a thief in this sexually tinged movie was simply unacceptable. Thus, the former Grace Kelly declined the role, although she told Hitchcock, "I hate disappointing you."

With the princess literally out of the picture, Hitchcock turned once more to Tippi Hedren. While some critics had belittled her performance in *The Birds*, the director still had faith in her, believing she might yet become a major star. The male lead, meanwhile, went to a rising young actor with strong box-office potential—Sean Connery, the virile Scotsman who was thrilling audiences in the new James Bond movies. Unfortunately, the high hopes that Hitchcock had for the film soon turned sour.

A psychological drama about a troubled woman, *Marnie* was made under troubled conditions. Accounts vary about what happened. According to one version, Hitchcock (rather like James Stewart's character in *Vertigo*) became obsessively attached to Tippi Hedren, sending her presents and telling her that he dreamed about her. Matters came to a head when

Hitchcock allegedly made a blatant, lewd proposition to Hedren, and she spurned him. At this point, the two stopped speaking to each other. If Hitchcock wished to give her some direction, he did so through a third party, saying such things as, "Tell that girl to . . ." Hedren responded in the same way.

Another account suggests that while an ugly confrontation did occur on the *Marnie* set, the circumstances were

Paul Newman shares a laugh with Hitchcock on the set of Torn Curtain. *Such jolly moments were rare, however; neither the director nor the actor was especially happy about making the picture.*

somewhat different. According to this version, Hedren simply wanted to take a break for a few days, only to have Hitchcock refuse her request. The exasperated actress responded by sarcastically referring to the director's weight—and that, Hitchcock said, was something "no one is permitted to do." Whatever the truth, Hedren was eventually released from her contract with Hitchcock and never worked for him again.

For those involved in *Marnie*, the troubles behind the scenes might have been offset if the reviews and public response had been strong. Unfortunately, the film became one of Hitchcock's biggest commercial failures in years, and it was lambasted by many critics, including some who otherwise admired his work. "Pathetically old-fashioned and dismally naive . . . a major disappointment" were the words of one reviewer. Over the years, however, other critics have hailed *Marnie* as a misunderstood masterpiece, a sensitive drama about the need for love and its potential power for healing.

Fewer critics, however, leaped to defend the director's next two projects—the spy thrillers *Torn Curtain* (1966) and *Topaz* (1969). Indeed, their appearance left many people thinking that the great director's best years were behind him. Hitchcock may even have agreed with them, for neither film was a happy experience to make.

For *Torn Curtain*, a gifted writer, Irish novelist Brian Moore, was recruited for the screenplay, but unfortunately, the story—a Cold War melodrama about an American scientist's attempts to smuggle a weapons secret out of East Germany— was not his kind of material. Moore later admitted that the screenplay was mostly Hitchcock's work. With little real collaboration between writer and director, the result was not a tight script but a long, meandering mishmash. Moreover, Universal insisted that Hitchcock cast two major stars in the leads, Paul Newman and Julie Andrews. Their high salaries sent the budget soaring—something Hitchcock especially resented. During filming, Hitchcock's relations with the actors were chilly, and when Newman sent him a memo outlining problems in the script, the director was furious. Ironically, it was the star power of Newman and Andrews that helped save *Torn Curtain* from commercial failure. Despite its high cost of $5 million, it managed to make $6.5 million, thus showing a small profit.

Topaz, however, was a total disaster. Based on a best-selling novel by Leon Uris, it involved a spy plot at the heart of the 1962 Cuban missile crisis. Uris's own script proved unusable even as the cameras were ready to roll, and Hitchcock, in desperation, contacted Samuel Taylor, the screenwriter of *Vertigo*, for help. This time, however, Taylor was unable to save the film. The writer recalled that some scenes were written only hours before they were shot—a makeshift method of filmmaking that echoed Hitchcock's equally negative experiences with *The Paradine Case*.

In addition to the script problems, there were the logistical difficulties of shooting in far-flung locations (which, in addition to California, included Copenhagen and Paris) as well as lackluster casting. Unlike *Torn Curtain*, *Topaz* featured few performers familiar to American audiences; its lead was Austrian actor Frederick Stafford, who gave a stiff, lifeless performance. The finished film, generally roasted in the press, was dull, uninvolving, and an even bigger failure than *Marnie* had been.

Compounding Hitchcock's woes during this period was the loss of valued collaborators. *Marnie* was his final project with cinematographer Robert Burks and editor George Tomasini, who had both suffered untimely deaths: Burks was killed in a fire at his home, while Tomasini succumbed to a heart attack. Then, during preparations for *Torn Curtain*, the director locked horns with composer Bernard Herrmann. Hitchcock wanted something new and different for the soundtrack, and he felt that Herrmann's efforts for this movie sounded too much like his previous scores. So, after working together for more than a decade on eight films in a row, the two parted company for good. The music for *Torn Curtain* was reassigned to British composer John Addison.

These years might have gone better for Hitchcock if he had been able to make the films he wanted to make. In 1966, after finishing *Torn Curtain*, he worked with several writers on a script that was called, at different times, "Frenzy" and "Kaleidoscope." It was a dark story, set in New York, about a deformed serial killer. Hitchcock wanted to experiment with non-traditional filming techniques—such as using natural light and handheld cameras—that he admired in some of the new European films. He saw the proposed movie as a way to shake things up, to do something different. Universal, however, found the story too brutal and rejected the project. In its place, Hitchcock reluctantly agreed to direct *Topaz*.

During these same years, the film Hitchcock most wanted to make was an adaptation of *Mary Rose*, a 1920 play by James M. Barrie, who had also written *Peter Pan*. Hitchcock had fallen in love with the drama during its original London run and for years dreamed of filming it. *Mary Rose* was a delicate fantasy about a young bride who disappears on her honeymoon and then resurfaces many years later, as youthful as the day she vanished. The project got as far as a finished screenplay by Jay Presson Allen, but Universal executives' perception that it had only meager commercial potential kept it on the shelf. In fact, Hitchcock often claimed that the company bosses had expressly forbidden him to make *Mary Rose*.

Partly because of his age, partly because of studio resistance, Hitchcock had definitely slowed down. The thought of retiring, however, was altogether alien to him. Movies were his life, and he would continue making them for as long as he was able.

Fifty-three film canisters attest to Hitchcock's long career. After completing Family Plot *in 1976 the director planned to make another film, but his age and failing health prevented him from doing so.*

LAST YEARS AND LEGACY

By the late 1960s, even as Hitchcock's career seemed to be in decline, the body of work he had created over the past four decades was attracting some serious attention. No longer was he simply being recognized as a gifted entertainer; many film connoisseurs were now hailing him as one of the medium's great geniuses.

This kind of attention had actually begun in France a few years earlier among a group of young critics—later to become filmmakers themselves—who wrote for the publication *Cahiers du Cinema* ("Journal of Cinema"). Passionately devoted to film, these critics argued that the best American movies, far from being the impersonal products of a relentlessly commercial industry, in fact bore the individual stamps, both visual and thematic, of their directors. The finest Hollywood directors, they said, were *auteurs* (authors) as surely as were novelists, playwrights, composers, and other artists. Hitchcock became a special hero to these young Frenchmen.

During the 1960s, one of the critics-turned-directors, François Truffaut, began a series of interviews with Hitchcock that were eventually published in book form. In those conversations, Hitchcock talked about every film he had made up through *Torn Curtain*. He recounted dozens of production anecdotes and took special delight in describing the techniques and visual strategies he used in particular films. A popular work with movie buffs, Truffaut's book became one of the basic sources of information about Hitchcock's career.

Writers in other countries followed the French lead. In America, critics such as Andrew Sarris and Peter Bogdanovich (another filmmaker-to-be) wrote glowingly of Hitchcock's work. Bogdanovich even helped to arrange a special presentation of the director's films at the prestigious Museum of Modern Art in New York. Meanwhile, in England, a young scholar named Robin Wood wrote *Hitchcock's Films*, a book that remains the essential critical study of Hitchcock. For Wood, Hitchcock's cinematic mastery and his exploration, in film after film, of important and often disturbing themes gave ample evidence of his artistry. Especially important, in Wood's view, was the "therapeutic theme," in which the trials and traumas endured by the main character cure him or her of a particular weakness or flaw. Hitchcock's special genius, Wood argued, lay in his ability—through his creation of suspense and his use of subjective techniques—to make the viewer identify closely with the main characters and experience the same emotions they are feeling.

The attention Hitchcock was drawing in highbrow film circles was apparently not lost on Hollywood. After years of passing him over for directing Oscars—he was nominated five times but never won—the Academy of Motion Picture Arts and Sciences finally decided to give him a special prize. In 1968, he was named the winner of the Irving G. Thalberg Award in recognition of his "consistent high level of production achievement." After so many years of neglect by his peers, however, Hitchcock was unimpressed with the honor. His acceptance speech consisted of only two words: "Thank you." And then he walked off the stage.

By 1970, coming off a string of disappointing pictures, Hitchcock was determined to make a movie worthy of his reputation. But what to film? Early that year, he read the novel *Goodbye Picadilly, Farewell Leicester Square* by Arthur La Bern, which concerned a London serial murderer and the man wrongly tried for the crimes. The basic story seemed tailor-made for him, but the thought of filming in England put him off at first—at his age, overseas travel was harder on him than it once had been. He finally decided, however, that shooting in London would be a good idea. The film could actually be made more cheaply there than in Hollywood, and he would have an abundant supply of first-rate actors from which to draw.

To write the script for what would be called *Frenzy* (a title he had first considered for one of his unrealized projects of the late 1960s), Hitchcock sought out Anthony Shaffer, an English playwright whose latest work, *Sleuth*, was enjoying successful runs on both the New York and London stages. The scripting proceeded smoothly, and by summer 1971, filming in London was set to begin. An able cast—Jon Finch, Barry Foster, Anna Massey, Alec McCowan, Vivien Merchant, and Barbara Leigh-Hunt—was assembled for this thriller whose plot hearkened back to *The Lodger* and Hitchcock's earliest days in the British cinema.

Hitchcock delightedly set much of the action in Covent Garden, long renowned in London as a wholesale marketplace for fruits and vegetables. He recalled the neighborhood vividly from his childhood visits there with his father, and during filming, he even encountered an aging gentleman who claimed to remember William Hitchcock Sr. (Only three years later, Covent Garden would be turned into a cluster of small shops and restaurants. Thus, *Frenzy* would offer one of the last glimpses of this historic area when it still bustled with produce merchants.)

The filming of *Frenzy* went well at first, as Hitchcock's creative juices flowed in a way that they had not done in years. Then something occurred that terrified him. Alma, who had been staying with her husband at the luxurious Claridges Hotel, suffered a stroke and had to return to California. Any hint that Alma might be lost to him was unbearable, and those on the set noticed a marked change in his demeanor—from cheerful professionalism to anxiety and depression. And, perhaps not surprisingly, his consumption of food and alcohol increased sharply.

Still, the meticulous preparation Hitchcock and Shaffer had done, combined with the talent of the cast, paid off. The film, released during the late spring of 1972, proved to be one of the director's most self-assured works in years. A return to the "wrong man" theme, *Frenzy* focuses on Richard Blaney (Finch), an embittered, ill-tempered man whose ex-wife and girlfriend both fall victim to a mad killer who uses neckties to strangle London women. Although the circumstantial evidence all points to Blaney, the real killer is actually Blaney's best friend, a jovial fruit dealer named Bob Rusk (Foster). Rusk manages to frame Blaney, who is tried and imprisoned for the crimes. But Blaney escapes and, with a tire iron in hand, goes immediately to Rusk's flat, intending to kill him. He brutally beats a figure on Rusk's bed only to discover that it is not Rusk but the corpse of Rusk's latest victim. Inspector Oxford (McCowan), the Scotland Yard detective in charge of the case, arrives at the scene just moments ahead of Rusk, who shows up hauling a large trunk in which he intended to conceal his victim's body. "Mr. Rusk," the inspector remarks dryly as the film ends, "you're not wearing your tie."

In previous films, especially *Shadow of a Doubt* and *Strangers on a Train*, Hitchcock had exposed the dark desires of his protagonists, revealing these characters as mirror images—or doubles—of the villains. In *Frenzy*, he offers a new variation on this design. Alternating between bursts of rage and bouts of self-pity, Richard Blaney is the least sympathetic "hero" in all of Hitchcock's films. By contrast, Bob

Rusk is, at first glance, Blaney's opposite—a likable chap, seemingly good-natured and ready to help his friends. Yet Rusk is guilty, and Blaney is innocent. Or at least Blaney is innocent until the final scene, when he shows himself to be quite as capable of murder as Rusk. With *Frenzy*, Hitchcock took his flawed protagonist to the logical extreme. Pushed to the limit, Blaney is ready to act on the destructive impulses that had long been boiling near the surface of his personality.

In its treatment of sex and violence, *Frenzy* was the most graphic film that Hitchcock ever made, more so even than *Psycho*. With the establishment of a new motion picture rating system a few years earlier, movies had gotten considerably bolder, and Hitchcock was perhaps trying to prove that he could be as up to date as any director. Nudity appears in several scenes, and one sequence in particular—the rape-strangulation of Blaney's ex-wife—is shown in especially gruesome detail. Still another scene, in which Rusk tries to retrieve his tie pin from the hand of a corpse he has hidden in a sack of potatoes, is played for dark humor. *Frenzy* was, accordingly, given an "R" ("restricted") rating by the Motion Picture Association of America. Tellingly, Patricia Hitchcock O'Connell refused to let her daughters see it.

The world premiere of *Frenzy* was held on May 25, 1972, in London. Alma had by this time recovered sufficiently from her stroke to make the trans-Atlantic trip and join in the festivities. While Hitchcock's return to his native soil was hailed by many in the British press, some reviewers were quick to point out that *Frenzy* portrayed a London that no longer existed. Filled with old-fashioned bits of dialogue and quaint secondary characters, the film reflected not the modern city but the one that the director remembered from his youth.

Since its anachronisms were less apparent to viewers in the United States, *Frenzy* fared better with American critics. *New York Times* reviewer Vincent Canby said that Hitchcock's "advancing years" had only enriched his talent and called *Frenzy* "the first good movie about a sex murderer since

Most of Frenzy *was filmed on location in London's Covent Garden. Hitchcock's return to his native city drew a great deal of attention from the British press.*

Psycho." The director, determined to ensure that *Frenzy* succeeded, made countless publicity appearances on its behalf. His efforts paid off. Costing only $2 million to make, *Frenzy* quickly earned more than three times that amount.

Still giving no thought to retirement, Hitchcock was soon at work on a new project. In 1973 he acquired rights to another English novel, Victor Canning's *The Rainbird Pattern*, and asked Anthony Shaffer to adapt it. The director and screenwriter disagreed, however, over how the material should be treated. The novel was rather dark and somber in tone, qualities that Shaffer wanted to preserve. Hitchcock favored a different approach. Apparently, after the grim brutality of *Frenzy*, he was ready to switch gears.

What attracted Hitchcock to *The Rainbird Pattern* was not its tone but its structure. Canning's book revolves around two distinctly different couples—a female psychic and her boyfriend and a pair of kidnappers (also a man and a woman). The psychic is hired by a wealthy dowager, Julia Rainbird, to find the long-missing heir to her family fortune. That search, in which the psychic involves her boyfriend, alternates with the daring exploits of the kidnappers. As the story progresses, we realize that the male kidnapper is in fact the Rainbird heir, the object of the other couple's search. Eventually, the psychic's investigation leads her to this dangerous criminal, who kills her. Hitchcock liked the way the book juggled the two stories and gradually brought them together. But feeling that the story would work better as a comedy, he insisted on a light tone and a happy ending. When he sensed that Shaffer was unwilling to give him what he wanted, he hired Ernest Lehman, the screenwriter of *North by Northwest*, as a replacement.

Hitchcock and Lehman began holding script conferences late in 1973, and by the middle of the following year, they had worked out much of the plot and many of the characterizations. But Hitchcock's health delayed the completion of the script. Late that year, chest pains and dizzy spells began plaguing him so severely that his doctors decided to implant a pacemaker in his chest to regulate his heart beat. He was still recovering from that procedure when he had to be treated for colitis and a kidney stone. Shooting, which had originally been set to begin in January 1975, was postponed until March.

Alhough Canning's novel was set in England, Hitchcock and Lehman found it easy enough to transpose the events to the United States. Shooting took place in San Francisco and at Universal Studios. Hitchcock had originally thought of using a cast of big names but decided, for economic reasons, on a less stellar but quite capable cast that included Bruce Dern, Barbara Harris, Karen Black, and William Devane. Not surprisingly, given the state of his health, the production was something of a trial for the director. As those on the set recalled, at some points he was alert to the tiniest of technical details, while at other times he seemed utterly weary of the process. "Bruce," he told his leading man at one point, "wake me when the movie's over."

Filming was nearly completed before the movie had a final title. *Deception*, *Deceit*, and *One Plus One Equals One* were among the possibilities considered. Finally, a member of the Universal publicity department suggested *Family Plot*, and that seemed appropriate, as the story involved intrigue within families and key bits of action occurred in cemeteries. It was released under that title in the spring of 1976. Its premiere was held on March 21 to mark the opening night of the Los Angeles International Film Exposition (Filmex). The organizers of the event named Hitchcock the recipient of the first-ever Filmex Award.

Family Plot met with generally warm, if not overly enthusiastic, reviews. "A witty, relaxed lark" was how Canby described it in the *New York Times*. Many reviewers noted its hair-raising set piece—a scene in which the Harris and Dern characters go careening down a mountain road in a car whose brakes have been sabotaged—and declared that Hitchcock had not lost his touch. A few critics, however, found the film overlong and uninspired.

The few years remaining to Hitchcock after *Family Plot* were not especially happy ones. His health—and that of Alma—continued to decline. Always a loner, he saw few people outside of those he encountered on the Universal grounds. Still, he insisted on going about script preparations for a new film to be entitled "The Short Night." At first he enlisted Ernest Lehman as the screenwriter but then replaced him with David Freeman, who was well known in Hollywood as a "script doctor" (a writer who revises problematical screenplays). The proposed film was a spy thriller inspired by a real-life case in Britain. Like *Topaz*, its locales hopped all over the globe—from England to New York to Finland—and given the director's medical condition, it is hard to imagine how he would have been able to endure the production.

Freeman later described his months of working with Hitchcock in a book he called *The Last Days of Alfred Hitchcock*; the book includes the final draft of the script for "The Short Night." Freeman's description of this collaboration paints a sad picture of a filmmaker suffering from arthritis and a heart ailment, drinking too much (in part to dull his physical pain), and desperately lonely. There were still more honors during this period—a knighthood from Queen Elizabeth II, a Lifetime Achievement Award from the American Film Institute (AFI)—but according to Freeman, such attention depressed Hitchcock more than it flattered him: "As far as he was concerned, they were preparing his obituary, and he didn't care to come to the funeral." Still, in the public appearances that accompanied these honors, Hitchcock managed to display his trademark humor and irony. When asked, for instance, why he thought it had taken the queen so long to get around to knighting him, Sir Alfred replied, "I suppose it was carelessness."

A U.S. postage stamp issued in 1998. The drawing in the upper lefthand corner of the stamp is Hitchcock's own rendering of his famous profile and was his longtime trademark.

After the AFI tribute in March 1979, he closed down his offices at Universal. He had made a valiant effort to keep working, but now he was only too aware that "The Short Night" would never become a movie. A year later, again in March, he made his last public appearance, taping a brief introduction to the ceremony for that year's AFI honoree: James Stewart, a veteran of four of Hitchcock's films, including two of his greatest, *Rear Window* and *Vertigo*.

Barely a month after that, on the morning of April 29, 1980, Alfred Hitchcock died quietly and at home on Bellagio Road. He was just three and a half months shy of his 81st birthday. Alma, his life's partner and closest advisor, died two years later.

In the two decades since his death, Hitchcock's work continues to spark close scrutiny among scholars and critics. Even before he died, his work was being taught regularly in college-level film courses, and today he remains probably the single most "studied" director in cinema history. Countless critical works, in the form of essays and books, have analyzed the nuances of his films from all kinds of perspectives. Many focus on his major themes and brilliant technical strategies. Still others explore his films for what they reveal about Hollywood filmmaking practices or about Anglo-American society, politics, and culture. One of the key questions many recent critics have pondered concerns Hitchcock's attitude toward women. Do such works as *Psycho* and *Frenzy*, both of which depict shocking acts of violence against female characters, reveal a man with a mean-spirited distrust or even hatred of the opposite sex? Such questions become complicated, however, when one considers how often in his films—from *The 39 Steps* to *Rear Window* to *North by Northwest*—an alliance with a strong, risk-taking woman helps save the hero's skin.

Paralleling the fascination that Hitchcock holds for so many critics and movie buffs is the influence he exerts over other directors. Brian De Palma, for instance, seemed to devote much of his early career to making films that echoed the master: *Sisters*, *Obsession*, *Dressed to Kill*, *Blow-Out*, and *Body Double* are all self-consciously "Hitchcockian" in both their techniques and their plots. When questioned about such borrowings, De Palma said that Hitchcock had pioneered "the grammar of cinema," suggesting that he was drawn to the older director's work because "I think film is a graphic art form." Other directors, Martin Scorsese and Steven Spielberg among them, have cited Hitchcock as a key influence, although their films may not show it as obviously as De Palma's do.

Over the years, there have been various remakes of Hitchcock classics. In 1998 alone, there were Andrew Davis's *A Perfect Murder* (a remake of *Dial "M" for Murder*), a made-for-TV *Rear Window*, and Gus Van Sant's *Psycho*. The last was the oddest example of all, since Van Sant reused Joseph Stefano's original screenplay and attempted to duplicate most of Hitchcock's scenes almost shot for shot. That it failed, quite spectacularly, to duplicate the original *Psycho*'s box-office success suggested, for more than one reviewer, that Hitchcock is truly inimitable.

In fact, there is no substitute for the real thing. In 1984, five Hitchcock films that, for legal reasons, had not been seen for years in theaters or on television, were re-released to great acclaim: *Rope*, *Vertigo*, the second version of *The Man Who Knew Too Much*, *Rear Window*, and *The Trouble with Harry*. Two of these films have since undergone restoration. A team of dedicated film preservationists, headed by Robert Harris and James Katz, went back to the studio vaults, retrieved the original negatives and soundtrack recordings for *Vertigo* and *Rear Window*, and restored these deteriorating films to their former glory. The restored *Vertigo* was shown in 1996; *Rear Window* followed in 2000.

Also, during the spring and summer of 1999, in honor of the 100th anniversary of the director's birth, New York's Museum of Modern Art mounted a major exhibition of Hitchcock memorabilia, along with screenings of all his films. Meanwhile, Hitchcock movies typically occupy their own section in video rental stores and have become staples of such cable television channels as American Movie Classics and Turner Classic Movies.

Alfred Hitchcock was a giant in world cinema for much of the 20th century. His legacy shows every sign of remaining strong well into the 21st.

CHRONOLOGY

August 13, 1899
Alfred Joseph Hitchcock is born in Leytonstone, England

1910
Enrolls in St. Ignatius College, London

1913
Leaves St. Ignatius; enrolls in courses at University of London

1915
Hired by Henley Telegraph and Cable Company

1919–20
Prepares title cards part-time for the London branch of Famous Players–Lasky, which later hires him for full-time position

1923
Works as assistant director on films produced by Michael Balcon

1925
Begins directing career with *The Pleasure Garden*, filmed in Germany and produced by Balcon

December 2, 1926
Marries Alma Lucy Reville

1927
The Lodger is released to great acclaim; begins directing films for John Maxwell and British International Pictures

July 7, 1928
Only child, Patricia, is born

1933–36
Reunites with Michael Balcon for several features, including *The Man Who Knew Too Much* and *The 39 Steps*

1938
Signs contract with American producer David O. Selznick; *The Lady Vanishes* is a major success

1939
Moves to United States to direct *Rebecca* for Selznick

1940
Begins directing films for other producers in "loan-out" arrangements with Selznick.

1941
Rebecca wins Academy Award as Best Picture of 1940

1947–49
Ends ties to Selznick with *The Paradine Case*; in partnership with Sidney Bernstein, directs *Rope* and *Under Capricorn* for the short-lived Transatlantic Pictures; signs multipicture contract with Warner Bros.

1953
Signs new deal with Paramount for several features, beginning with *Rear Window*

1955
Becomes American citizen on April 20; begins hosting *Alfred Hitchcock Presents*; directs remake of *The Man Who Knew Too Much*

1960
Psycho becomes a smash hit

1962
Settles at Universal Pictures, which will release the remainder of his films; directs *The Birds*

1968
Receives Irving G. Thalberg Award from the Academy of Motion Picture Arts and Sciences

1971
Films *Frenzy* in London

1976
Hitchcock's final film, *Family Plot*, is released

1978–79
Receives Lifetime Achievement Award from the American Film Institute and a knighthood from Queen Elizabeth II

April 29, 1980
Dies at home in Bel-Air

FURTHER READING

BIOGRAPHICAL WORKS AND GENERAL BOOKS ABOUT HITCHCOCK

Auiler, Dan. *Hitchcock's Notebooks: An Authorized and Illustrated Look Inside the Creative Mind of Alfred Hitchcock.* New York: Spike, 1999.

———. *Vertigo: The Making of a Hitchcock Classic.* New York: St. Martin's, 1998.

DeRosa, Steven. *Writing with Hitchcock: The Collaboration of Alfred Hitchcock and John Michael Hayes.* New York: Faber & Faber, 2001.

Finler, Joel W. *Hitchcock in Hollywood.* New York: Continuum, 1992.

Freeman, David. *The Last Days of Alfred Hitchcock.* Woodstock, N.Y.: Overlook Press, 1984.

Gottlieb, Sidney, ed. *Hitchcock on Hitchcock: Selected Writings and Interviews.* Berkeley: University of California Press, 1995.

Hunter, Evan. *Me and Hitch.* London: Faber and Faber, 1997.

Kapsis, Robert E. *Hitchcock: The Making of a Reputation.* Chicago: University of Chicago Press, 1992.

Krohn, Bill. *Hitchcock at Work.* London: Phaidon, 2000.

Leff, Leonard J. *Hitchcock and Selznick: The Rich and Strange Collaboration of Alfred Hitchcock and David O. Selznick.* 1987. Reprint, Berkeley: University of California Press, 1999.

Leigh, Janet, with Christopher Hickens. *Psycho: Behind the Scenes of the Classic Thriller.* New York: Harmony Books, 1995.

Mogg, Ken. *The Alfred Hitchcock Story.* Dallas: Taylor, 1999.

Rebello, Stephen. *Alfred Hitchcock and the Making of Psycho.* 1990. Reprint, New York: St. Martin's, 1999.

Ryall, Tom. *Alfred Hitchcock and the British Cinema.* Urbana: University of Illinois Press, 1986.

Sloan, Jane E. *Alfred Hitchcock: A Filmography and Bibliography.* 1993. Reprint, Berkeley: University of California Press, 1995.

Spoto, Donald. *The Dark Side of Genius: The Life of Alfred Hitchcock.* 1983. Reprint, New York: Da Capo, 1999.

Taylor, John Russell. *Hitch: The Life and Times of Alfred Hitchcock.* 1978. Reprint, New York: Da Capo, 1996.

INTERVIEWS WITH HITCHCOCK

Bogdanovich, Peter. *Who the Devil Made It*. New York: Alfred A. Knopf, 1997. A hefty compendium of the author's conversations with 16 directors, including Hitchcock.

Schickel, Richard. *The Men Who Made the Movies*. 1975. Reprint, Chicago: Ivan R. Dee, 2001. Transcripts of filmed interviews with eight directors, including Hitchcock, which were originally conducted for the public television series of the same name.

Truffaut, François, in collaboration with Helen G. Scott. *Hitchcock*. 1967. Rev. ed., New York: Simon & Schuster, 1984.

SELECTED CRITICAL WORKS

Rohmer, Eric, and Claude Chabrol. *Hitchcock: The First Forty-four Films*. Translated by Stanley Hochman. New York: Frederick Unger, 1979.

Spoto, Donald. *The Art of Alfred Hitchcock: Fifty Years of His Motion Pictures*. 2nd ed., New York: Anchor, 1992.

Sterritt, David. *The Films of Alfred Hitchcock*. New York: Cambridge University Press, 1993.

Wood, Robin. *Hitchcock's Films Revisited*. New York: Columbia University Press, 1989. Includes the full text of Wood's original *Hitchcock's Films* (1965) as well as assorted essays on the director that Wood wrote in later years.

ABOUT HOLLYWOOD AND THE MOVIES

Nowell-Smith, Geoffrey, ed. *The Oxford History of World Cinema*. New York: Oxford University Press, 1996.

Sarris, Andrew. *"You Ain't Heard Nothin' Yet": The American Talking Film, History and Memory, 1927–1948*. New York: Oxford University Press, 1998.

Schatz, Thomas. *The Genius of the System: Hollywood Filmmaking in the Studio Era*. New York: Pantheon, 1988.

FILMS DIRECTED BY ALFRED HITCHCOCK

SILENT FILMS

The Pleasure Garden. Gainsborough-Emelka, 1925.
The Mountain Eagle. Gainsborough-Emelka, 1927.
The Lodger: A Story of the London Fog. Gainsborough, 1927.
Downhill. Gainsborough, 1927.
Easy Virtue. Gainsborough, 1927.
The Ring. British International Pictures, 1927.
Champagne. British International Pictures, 1928.
The Farmer's Wife. British International Pictures, 1928.
The Manxman. British International Pictures, 1929.

SOUND FILMS

Blackmail. British International Pictures, 1929.
Juno and the Paycock. British International Pictures, 1930.
Murder! British International Pictures, 1930.
The Skin Game. British International Pictures, 1931.
Number Seventeen. British International Pictures, 1932.
Rich and Strange. British International Pictures, 1932.
Waltzes from Vienna. Tom Arnold Productions, 1934.
The Man Who Knew Too Much. Gaumont-British, 1934.
The 39 Steps. Gaumont-British, 1935.
Secret Agent. Gaumont-British, 1936.
Sabotage. Gaumont-British, 1936.
Young and Innocent. Gaumont-British, 1938.
The Lady Vanishes. Gaumont-British, 1938.
Jamaica Inn. Mayflower Pictures, 1939.
Rebecca. Selznick International Pictures, 1940.
Foreign Correspondent. Walter Wanger Productions/United Artists, 1940.
Mr. & Mrs. Smith. RKO, 1941.
Suspicion. RKO, 1941.
Saboteur. Universal, 1942.
Shadow of a Doubt. Universal, 1943.
Lifeboat. 20th Century-Fox, 1944.
Spellbound. Selznick International Pictures, 1945.
Notorious. RKO, 1946.
The Paradine Case. Selznick International Pictures/Vanguard, 1947.
Rope. Transatlantic Pictures, 1948.
Under Capricorn. Transatlantic Pictures, 1949.

Stage Fright. Warner Bros., 1950.
Strangers on a Train. Warner Bros., 1951.
I Confess. Warner Bros., 1953.
Dial "M" for Murder. Warner Bros., 1954.
Rear Window. Paramount, 1954.
To Catch a Thief. Paramount, 1955.
The Trouble with Harry. Paramount, 1955.
The Man Who Knew Too Much. Paramount, 1956.
The Wrong Man. Warner Bros., 1956.
Vertigo. Paramount, 1958.
North by Northwest. MGM, 1959.
Psycho. Paramount, 1960.
The Birds. Universal, 1963.
Marnie. Universal, 1964.
Torn Curtain. Universal, 1966.
Topaz. Universal, 1969.
Frenzy. Universal, 1972.
Family Plot. Universal, 1976.

INDEX

ACKNOWLEDGMENTS

For several years during my childhood, I thought that Alfred Hitchcock was just that funny fellow who introduced those creepy stories on television every week. Only gradually did I become aware of him as a great film director. Eventually my interest in his movies would border on the obsessive, and after I entered the graduate program in film studies at Columbia University in the late 1970s, it was an easy decision to choose his work as the subject of my master's thesis.

At Columbia in those days, Hitchcock was a hero--the school had awarded him an honorary doctorate in 1972. I went there expecting immersion in the Master of Suspense, and I got it. Three professors, in particular, immeasurably deepened my appreciation for Hitchcock's films: Andrew Sarris, John Belton (now of Rutgers University), and Stefan Sharff. I remain grateful to them to this day.

I could not have written this book without help from others. My friend Scot Danforth read an early version of the manuscript and offered valuable insight and encouragement. Brigit Dermott, project editor at Oxford University Press, guided the book toward publication with skill and good cheer. Nancy Toff, editorial director of Trade and Young Adult Reference at Oxford, allowed me to undertake this labor of love in the first place, and for that she deserves special thanks.

Most of all, I am grateful to my wife, Leslie, who read the manuscript, watched many an old Hitchcock movie with me, and supported me throughout the entire process.

PICTURE CREDITS

Courtesy of the Academy of Motion Picture Arts and Sciences: 77, 94; Bibliothèque du Film: 98; British Film Institute: 10, 15, 20, 23, 36, 41, 46, 49, 56, 60, 62, 112; Canal Plus Image: 36; Reprinted with permission of the Hitchcock Estate: 10, 15, 29, 41, 62; National Postal Museum, Smithsonian Institute/Stamp Design © 1998 U.S. Postal Service: 145; Photofest: cover, 2, 7, 65, 71, 74, 86, 96, 108, 118, 124, 132, 136, 146; Vestry House Museum: 13, 29

TEXT CREDITS

p. 30: From Shickel, Richard. *The Men Who Made the Movies* (Chicago: Ivan R. Dee, 2001), 280–81. Courtesy Thirteen/WNET New York

p. 52: From Shickel, Richard. *The Men Who Made the Movies* (Chicago: Ivan R. Dee, 2001), 293–94. Courtesy Thirteen/WNET New York

p. 100: From *Hitchcock on Hitchcock: Selected Writings and Interviews,* ed. Sidney Gottlieb (Berkeley: University of California Press, 1995), 210–26. Reprinted with permission from the Encyclopaedia Britannica, 14th ed., vol. 15, 1965 by Encyclopaedia Britannica, Inc.

p. 125: From *Hitchcock on Hitchcock: Selected Writings and Interviews,* ed. Sidney Gottlieb (Berkeley: University of California Press, 1995), 54–58. Courtesy of the Hitchcock Trust.

Gene Adair, who has worked in publishing since 1981, is currently the marketing manager at the University of Tennessee Press. A former teacher and newspaper reporter, he is also the author of young adult biographies of George Washington Carver and Thomas Alva Edison. He holds a Master of Fine Arts in film studies from Columbia Univesity.